Story S-t-r-e-t-c-h-e-r-s for Infants, Toddlers, and Twos

STORY
S-t-r-e-t-c-h-e-r-s®
for
Infants, Toddlers, and Twos

Experiences, Activities, and Games
for Popular Children's Books

Shirley Raines, Karen Miller, and Leah Curry-Rood

Illustrated by Kathy Dobbs

gryphon house
Beltsville, MD

Dedication

From Shirley Raines

To Miss Elizabeth Jackson, a teacher who inspired me
To Irene and Athel Raines, the parents who guided me
To Brian, who lets me remember him as a child
To Bob, who loves all readers
In memory and honor of all those who taught us to "love a good story"

From Karen Miller

To Dillon and Grace, the newest babies in my family. May you become avid
readers and have fine stories to tell!

From Leah Curry-Rood

This book is dedicated to all of the people who have devoted themselves to
ensuring the creation of good books for children. Special thanks go to
Susan Hirschman, Skip Dye, Bill Morris, Joe Boyd, Jazaan Higgins,
Mimi Kayden, Phillip Lee, Kathy Baxter, Marjorie Naughton, Anita
Silvey, Jennifer McCluskey, Kathy Neumann, Richard Robinson, Jeannie
Lybecker, and Isabel Baker. These people have worked tirelessly to
develop quality books for children, and to make them available
everywhere. Without their commitment and perseverance, children's
books and children's publishing would be very different. I would also
like to dedicate this book to Cindy Allen, for all of her efforts on the
Story Stretcher books.

Copyright © 2002, Shirley Raines, Karen Miller, and Leah Curry-Rood

Published by Gryphon House, Inc., 10726 Tucker Street, Beltsville, MD 20705 or
P.O. Box 207, Beltsville, MD 20704-0207.
(800) 638-0928, (301) 595-9500, (301) 595-0051 (Fax)

Visit us on the web at www.gryphonhouse.com

Illustrations: Kathy Dobbs

Library of Congress Cataloging-in-Publication Data

Raines, Shirley C.
  Story stretchers for infants, toddlers, and twos : experiences and
ideas to expand books for children under three / Shirley Raines, Karen
Miller, and Leah Curry-Rood ; illustrations, Katheryn Davis.
    p. cm.
Includes bibliographical references (p.   ) and index.
  ISBN 0-87659-274-4
  1. Early childhood education--Activity programs. 2. Children--Books
and reading. I. Miller, Karen, 1942- II. Curry-Rood, Leah. III. Title.
LB1139.35.A37 R354 2002
372.4--dc21
                                    2002004803

Bulk purchase

Gryphon House books are
available for special premium
and sales promotions as well as
for fund-raising use. Special
editions or book excerpts also
can be created to specification.
For details, contact the Director
of Sales at the phone number or
address on this page.

Disclaimer

The publisher and the authors
cannot be held responsible for
injury, mishap, or damages
incurred during the use of or
because of the information in
this book. The authors
recommend appropriate
supervision of children at all
times.

From Collaboration to Partnership to Friendship

Leah Curry-Rood, one of the three authors of *Story S-t-r-e-t-c-h-e-r-s for Infants, Toddlers, and Twos: Experiences, Activities, and Games for Popular Children's Books*, introduced Karen Miller and me. I had admired Karen's writing and her abilities to hold an audience spellbound with her stories of teachers and children. Admiring one from afar and forming a writing partnership are different perspectives. Leah, with her love of people and her drive to publish quality teacher resources, started the collaboration that grew to a partnership and ended with a friendship. I shall always be grateful for Leah's introduction. Karen Miller knows children, caregivers' concerns, and parents' hopes and dreams.

Passionate about children, committed to quality early childhood education, dedicated to developing a love of literature in childhood, and enthusiastic about publishing exceptional teacher resources are descriptions of Leah Curry-Rood. Leah is known in the industry for her expertise, but as authors we know her for her passions. It is with great pride that Leah Curry-Rood's name graces the cover of this *Story S-t-r-e-t-c-h-e-r* book. She has been a collaborator, partner, and friend in the production of the four other *Story S-t-r-e-t-c-h-e-r* books, especially with helping to make the book selections for the other *Story S-t-r-e-t-c-h-e-r* books in the series.

Karen Miller, Leah Curry-Rood, and I have grown from collaborators to partners to friends in the process of writing *Story S-t-r-e-t-c-h-e-r-s for Infants, Toddlers, and Twos: Experiences, Activities, and Games for Popular Children's Books*. However, our work together could not have flourished without the guidance of Kathy Charner. Kathy's editorial expertise, her insights, and her shared vision for the book guided us. Thank you, Kathy. And, the final touch, the beautiful pages you are reading were designed by Mike Freeman and Rosanna Demps. Thank you, Mike and Rosanna.

Table of Contents

Introduction

Books and young children are a natural combination. Children love to have stories read to them and told to them. They love the ideas, pictures, and characters in the stories. Whether it is a toddler's favorite book, *If You Were My Bunny* by Kate McMillan, a two-year-old's favorite *Max* book by Rosemary Wells, or an infant's favorite game, *Peekaboo, Baby!* by Denise Lewis Patrick, infants, toddlers, and twos delight in interacting with adults and stories. These adult-child-book interactions are positive forces for children's emerging literacy. Parents, teachers, and caregivers who engage in this lovely triad (adult-child-book interaction) are setting the stage for children to learn to read. However, more than the promise of later literacy, story and book interactions provide emotional bonding, language stimulation, and cognitive development. All of the books featured in *Story S-t-r-e-t-c-h-e-r-s for Infants, Toddlers, and Twos: Experiences, Activities, and Games for Popular Children's Books* were selected because we know children enjoy them for their stories or for their interactive content possibilities. The complexity of learning, the value of interactions, and development of language are explored with the children's books featured in *Story S-t-r-e-t-c-h-e-r-s for Infants, Toddlers, and Twos.*

Why We Wrote This Book

Story S-t-r-e-t-c-h-e-r-s for Infants, Toddlers, and Twos was written at the request of hundreds of teachers, caregivers, parents, grandparents, and librarians. The four previous *Story S-t-r-e-t-c-h-e-r* books, which focused on books for preschoolers and children in the early elementary grades, have been very popular with early childhood educators. Two of the many features these educators appreciate are the quality of the children's books that are featured and the curriculum extension ideas (the story s-t-r-e-t-c-h-e-r-s). After many conference presentations, professionals and parents of children under three asked Shirley Raines to write a *Story S-t-r-e-t-c-h-e-r* book they could use with their children. Similar requests have followed Karen Miller's presentations as author of *Simple Steps: Developmental Activities for Infants, Toddlers, and Two-Year-Olds.* Teachers and parents want more information about children's development and appropriate activities. As an authority on

children's literature and as a major publisher of early childhood teacher resource books, Leah Curry-Rood often hears the same requests: "Give us more books about infants, toddlers, and twos." Finally, we have a new book: *Story S-t-r-e-t-c-h-e-r-s for Infants, Toddlers, and Twos: Experiences, Activities, and Games for Popular Children's Books.*

The Book Format

We wrote *Story S-t-r-e-t-c-h-e-r-s for Infants, Toddlers, and Twos* to support adults who want to provide a *print-rich* and *literature-rich* environment for young children. To help the reader do so, this book contains a selection of excellent books and ideas—or story s-t-r-e-t-c-h-e-r-s—to use with infants, toddlers, twos, and an extensive annotated bibliography of books that are appropriate for children under the age of three.

In Chapter 1, we discuss young children's development, emerging literacy, and what makes a book *good*. Chapter 2 provides a selection of good books for infants, hints for using the books, and the story s-t-r-e-t-c-h-e-r-s that accompany each featured book. Chapter 3 provides the same for toddlers, and Chapter 4 for two-year-olds. Chapter 5 offers an annotated bibliography of other books that we recommend. The book contains five indexes for easy reference: author and illustrator; book titles; bindings; type of story s-t-r-e-t-c-h-e-r, such as sensory or language; and materials.

For each of the featured children's books in Chapters 2, 3, and 4 there is a two-page spread that includes:

- the cover of the book,
- a Story Synopsis,
- Reading Hints,
- three Story S-t-r-e-t-c-h-e-r-s, and
- Something to Think About.

Photographs of children and illustrations of story s-t-r-e-t-c-h-e-r-s (the book-related activities) grace each two-page spread. The story s-t-r-e-t-c-h-e-r-s are from the following areas:

- language
- movement
- music
- object play

- pretending, and
- sensory.

Each book section ends with *Something to Think About*, which may highlight children's development, the significance of the suggested interactions, or additional ways the adult might s-t-r-e-t-c-h the concept.

What Is a Story S-t-r-e-t-c-h-e-r?

A story s-t-r-e-t-c-h-e-r is an interactive teaching idea based on the story or content in a children's book. The story s-t-r-e-t-c-h-e-r is designed for active participation, for doing, for manipulating objects, and for learning about concepts. The activities are fun and are guided by what we know about young children as learners.

What Makes a Book S-t-r-e-t-c-h-a-b-l-e?

A good story s-t-r-e-c-h-e-r book is one that introduces or develops concepts, connects to what children already know, provides opportunities for fun, or that interests children with its story, design, or format. For example, *Pretty Brown Face* helps to build the concept of a positive self-image. *Here Are My Hands* connects with what children already know about their bodies. Singing *Roll Over* while reading the book by Merle Peek is just plain fun! *Pat the Bunny*'s design invites children to touch and experience the book. All of these books are enjoyable as books, and they stimulate teachable ideas and activities. They can be s-t-r-e-t-c-h-e-d into different areas of child-adult interactions.

Not all books are meant to be s-t-r-e-t-c-h-e-d. Some should be enjoyed for their own sake, rather than for a connection that can be made to a teachable concept or an activity associated with the story. Sometimes a book should be enjoyed alone. Other times a book can be followed immediately with the activity or s-t-r-e-t-c-h-e-r. As the adult in the situation, you must observe the child's interactions and decide when or whether to proceed with an associated s-t-r-e-t-c-h-e-r (activity).

What Are Appropriate Story S-t-r-e-t-c-h-e-r-s for Infants, Toddlers, and Twos?

Developmentally appropriate activities for infants, toddlers, and twos depend on the age, developmental level, and background experiences of the children, as well as what the adult brings to the interaction. Examples for infants include Mirror Fun (page 72) from *Pretty Brown Face* by Andrea and Brian Pickney and Show Me Your Nose (page 78) from *Show Me!* by Nadine Bernard Westcott. Examples for toddlers include Animal Collection (page 142) from *This Is the Farmer* by Nancy Tafuri and Hand Prints (page 115) from *Here Are My Hands* by Bill Martin, Jr. and John Archambault. Examples for two-year-olds include Go-Together Collection (page 205) from *Some Things Go Together* by Charlotte Zolotow and Animal Sounds (page 203) from *Seals on the Bus* by Lenny Hort.

How to Use This Book

To use *Story S-t-r-e-t-c-h-e-r-s for Infants, Toddlers, and Twos* effectively, begin by reading the introduction to the chapters that describe the age of the children in your group—infants, toddlers, or two-year-olds. Select a book featured in that chapter that you think may capture children's interest. Read the book yourself and imagine how the children will receive the book. Review the story s-t-r-e-t-c-h-e-r-s written especially for the book you selected. Choose one story s-t-r-e-t-c-h-e-r to do on the day you read the book or the day after, depending on the interests and abilities of the children. Collect the materials you will need and follow the directions while also following the lead of the children. Children enjoy the repetition of books and the reassurance of the sameness of the text and the illustrations, so sharing the same book on another day or again in the same sitting is appropriate.

Once you understand how to make connections between the book and the children, try story s-t-r-e-t-c-h-e-r-s with a new, less familiar, book. You will look forward to sharing a story and sharing the fun while you help children develop sensory awareness, language development, and creative thinking.

Story S-t-r-e-t-c-h-e-r-s for Infants, Toddlers, and Twos is a resource book. It can be used as written, and it also lends itself to modification so activities can be changed to fit individual interests and abilities. The materials needed to s-t-r-e-t-c-h the books are familiar and easy to find. For safety purposes, always supervise children as they interact with materials suggested in the activity. Put materials away after you do a s-t-r-e-t-c-h-e-r so children use the materials only when you are with them. In addition, materials should always be reviewed for suitability for the specific children who will use them. If you question whether a child can use any material safely, it is best to choose another activity or modify the materials used. Check children's health records carefully for allergies. If you are in doubt, double check with the parents.

Summary

From our research on emerging literacy behaviors and from our experiences with children under three, we know that children who are read to and who interact with adults about books usually become good readers. We encourage you to use the ideas in *Story S-t-r-e-t-c-h-e-r-s for Infants, Toddlers, and Twos* to promote children's interest in books, to stimulate and expand their attention span, and to simply enjoy the fun of being together with a good book.

Chapter 1—From Language Development to Emerging Literacy

The connection between an early love of books and later success as a reader is well-documented. Language development and subsequent literacy development are inextricably connected. This chapter discusses the value of language development; offers guidance for selecting books for infants, toddlers, and twos; discusses ways to communicate with children about books; and discusses the importance of both text and illustrations in picture books for young children.

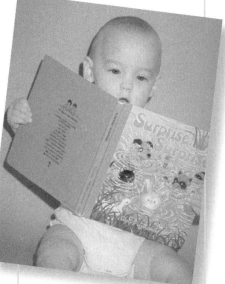

The Value of Language Development

In thinking about the earliest years of a child's life, it is important to ask, "What can we do with babies and young children that will be most important to their development?" The greatest resource we can share with young children is *language*. Talking, singing, storytelling, laughing, reading, and any other activity that involves spoken language should be our focus. Talking to babies and young children, and explaining what we are doing with them throughout the day, increases the number of words and sounds available to them and fosters their cognitive, emotional, social, and even physical development.

The importance of using spoken language with young children is such a simple concept that it is sometimes difficult to grasp. The value of a teacher who carefully builds loving relationships with children through the use of language is impossible to overestimate. Responding to children with explanations, asking questions about the day's experiences, and affirming children's understanding in a way that shows respect for them are essential skills for a teacher.

The value of a teacher who carefully builds loving relationships with children through the use of language is impossible to overestimate.

In addition to conversation, reading aloud is another way to stimulate early language. Many adults find that reading to young children is a comfortable way to begin early communication. Reading aloud to infants should happen early and often, several times a day. It is important to hold the baby while reading; this helps with relationship-building and creates a link between reading and secure, loving feelings, which is extremely important. Right from the start, the message is that reading is important and fun, and makes the child feel good.

Stages of Language Development

Watching the development of language in young children is truly inspiring! From day one, an infant tries to figure out this code that sets humans apart from other beings. Learning to talk is one of the true marvels of human development. Anyone who has tried to learn a foreign language knows how difficult it is. And yet, here are these tiny people who amaze us daily with the things that come out of their mouths.

Understanding language and talking are two different processes. Both require that a child hear well enough to distinguish meaningful sounds. Understanding is a sensory perception process sometimes called receptive language. A child will understand many words before using them in speech. Speaking is a cognitive and motor process—getting the muscles of the tongue and mouth to function together just right to produce the desired sound. This is often referred to as expressive language.

Studies show that a newborn is able to distinguish her mother's voice. A baby will stop random movements when she hears an interesting sound, as though she is concentrating. Soon, the baby responds by making eye contact or moving her mouth when another person talks to her face-to-face.

Crying and Random Sounds

Crying is a baby's first form of expressive language. It is an early piece of the communication process. When adults respond in a caring way, the baby discovers that making noises come out of her mouth is one way to make things happen and to get relief from distress. Soon the baby develops different cries for hunger, pain, rage, and boredom and a familiar caregiver learns to distinguish which is which. It's not long before the infant learns to cry to communicate.

Many adults find that reading to young children is a comfortable way to begin early communication.

When a baby is content, you hear random coos and gurgles. Enjoy getting into a real "conversation" with the baby, trading coos and other sounds. Imitate the sounds you hear the child making and take turns. This is one of the first skills in learning to communicate—to be quiet while someone else talks, and then to say something while the other person listens. This is an exciting social activity for the child, and you'll hear her practice these sounds on her own. More and more sounds will emerge with time.

Emerging Listening Skills

A baby under eight months of age will turn her head to locate the speaker visually and will often stop crying when someone speaks in a comforting way. She will respond to tone of voice. She may, for example, be frightened by angry intonations or smile at a happy voice.

Babbling and Jargon

Repetition of syllables is such fun to hear! At two or three months, babies start with just two or three repetitions of a sound such as "ma, ma, ma." As time goes on, the child may mix several different sounds. Later, she will demonstrate that she has learned one of the most basic elements of communication—intonation, the melody of language. She will make simple vowel sounds and play with pitch and rhythm. She will laugh and squeal. When she is playing alone, you'll hear the jabber of a string of nonsense syllables that sound like actual speech. Her voice will go up and down as though she is asking questions or making demands. This is called "jargon speech."

Between four and eight months, the child enjoys a "cooing conversation," taking turns with an adoring adult. She learns to use speech sounds to get attention, show enthusiasm, or reject something.

Understanding Words

As the child approaches one year of age, she begins to understand the meanings of a few words, such as "bottle" and "bye-bye." She can understand simple phrases such as "come here," "sit down," and "don't touch" when used emphatically. She will respond to her own name, and can turn and point to familiar people and a few familiar objects.

Between four and eight months, the child enjoys a "cooing conversation," taking turns with an adoring adult.

Talking to young children helps shape the brain for language.

Saying Single Words

Toward the end of the first year, a baby may start to say single words. She has discovered that specific sounds are attached to certain objects and actions. Not only does she realize that a certain combination of sounds represents a thing, but she learns how to move her lips, tongue, and mouth to produce sounds that others can interpret. Needless to say, this takes months of practice! That's what was going on with all the jabbering! The child may also try to echo words others say. "Dada," "Mama," "Hi," "Bye," and "No!" accompanied by gestures are among common first words. So is "Uh-oh!"

Telegraphic Speech

This usually occurs as a child approaches two. The child puts together two or three words, which sound like the old telegraph messages: "Want juice!"

Grammar

The acquisition of grammar—learning the rules of language—is a most interesting phenomenon. A two-year-old child will figure out a rule of grammar just from listening. For instance, she will learn to add the "s" sound to create a plural: "My shoes are wet." She may apply the grammar rule to new situations inappropriately: "My feets are wet." She may use "ed" to create past tense: "I danced all night." And she may transfer that rule to other situations: "I throwed the ball." Although the child is making "mistakes" in these phrases, the mistakes actually show thinking skills. In many ways, toddler grammar is more logical than the "correct" grammar they come to use later on. Depending on the child's language models, child-invented grammar is eventually replaced by the standard usage.

How to Develop Children's Language

It's quite simple: Talk to young children. Talking to them helps shape their brains for language. Talk about what is happening. Surround the child with an "envelope of language." Even with non-verbal infants, talk about what the child is seeing or doing at the moment. Be a "broadcaster." Just like a play-by-play announcer, describe what the child is doing, observing, and feeling.

All activities—planned, spontaneous, formal, and informal—are language activities. Infants do not need to be taught language.

They learn language naturally by hearing it used in context. They learn to talk by being talked to and listened to.

When a child starts to utter words and phrases, get down on her level and listen patiently as she tries to express herself. Instead of correcting mistakes in pronunciation or grammar, simply repeat the word or phrase correctly in your own sentence as a natural part of the conversation. "Yes, I see. Your *feet are* wet." Expand on what the child is talking about as that is engaging her at the moment. "Did you step in the puddle when we were outside?" Hearing language used meaningfully in daily routines is the most powerful "language lesson."

Language coming from television, even from so-called educational programs, has no value for very young children. These sounds are meaningless because the flickering shape on the screen is abstract and the speech is too rapid. Most teachers gear their speech to children, speaking slowly and clearly, getting children's full attention.

Remember that communication involves more than words. Understanding a child's attempts at communication means interpreting not only the sounds she makes, but also her facial expressions, gestures, intonations, and circumstances. Responsive care and kind words send a clear message that you are interested in what she is trying to communicate, that language serves a purpose. Successful affirmation of communication efforts is very important to the young child's language development.

When to Be Concerned
You may worry about a young child's mispronunciations, but these are the years when the child is just learning to manipulate sounds so there is usually no cause for concern. The following "red flags" may indicate a visit to a speech and hearing professional for an evaluation:

- The child is not using any words by two years of age.
- The child's speech cannot be understood by three years of age, with many consonant sounds omitted.
- The child is not using phrases of more than two or three words by the age of three.
- The child's speech and sounds are very harsh or nasal.
- The child has a history of recurrent ear infections, which could result in a hearing loss or language delay.

Hearing language used meaningfully in the routines of the day is the most powerful "language lesson."

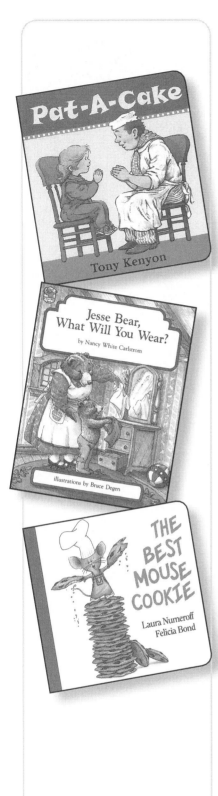

Early Literacy

A discussion of language development automatically leads to an examination of literacy—reading, in other words. We live in a society that relies heavily on the written word. Learning to interpret symbols to read and write is critical for success. In a broader sense, literacy refers to communication—the ability to give and receive information.

Teachers can develop literacy skills—pre-reading skills—in infants, toddlers, and two-year-olds by:

- Giving children interesting things to talk about and opportunities to express themselves.
- Telling them short stories.
- Exposing children to pictures and a variety of images (which are also symbols).
- Reading to them from age-appropriate picture books.
- Allowing them to handle books and use them freely as toys.
- Communicating the attitude that reading books is fun.
- Providing diverse experiences with people and places that will foster learning and increase children's understanding about the world.
- Making sure children are in good health, checking on potential hearing, vision, or speech problems that might prevent the normal development of pre-reading skills.

What About Teaching the ABC's?

Learning to sing the "ABC Song" has very little to do with learning how to read. Very young children have little need to know the sequence of the alphabet until they learn dictionary skills in elementary school. Many children's alphabet books and television shows try to teach children to recognize letters, and children impress adults by being able to point to a letter and name it. This is a very small step in learning to read. While it won't hurt children to learn letters, more important skills should be addressed at this age, such as increasing vocabulary and learning to speak in sentences.

Using Books with Infants, Toddlers, and Twos

Learning to love books is an important part of literacy and should begin in infancy. Helping infants acquire a natural love for books and stories is the number one literacy goal for the first year of a child's life. When you involve a child in looking at a bright picture book while warmly snuggled on your lap, the child absorbs the idea that reading is a *pleasurable* activity. Studies have shown that being read to in early childhood is highly influential in determining a child's success with learning to read in elementary school. When teachers and parents read to children often and with enthusiasm, children see reading as pleasurable, interesting, and worthwhile. They learn that books have a beginning, middle, and end, and that stories progress. They learn that the marks on the page have something to do with the pictures. On a more subtle level, children also learn the expectation that they too will learn to read because this is something people do.

Young toddlers enjoy the hinge action of sturdy board books. A toddler might turn a page back and forth over and over again. She is creating her own "peekaboo" experience, watching a picture appear and disappear over and over again. Sturdy cardboard pages also help the child learn to use her thumb and forefinger to turn the pages, a necessary skill for mastering paper pages.

Helping infants acquire a natural love for books and stories is the number one literacy goal for the first year of a child's life.

Make available a variety of different types of books. Bindings may be board, cloth, plastic, or paper. Rotate titles, putting some away and taking different ones out occasionally to keep interest high. As children explore books, they learn how books work and that looking at books is relaxing and comforting. They can then learn to find comfort and security with a collection of familiar books.

Young children can be taught to respect books, to turn the pages carefully, and to help put them away. Encourage them to help you put the books back on the shelf. If a book develops a tear, let the children watch while you repair it with tape. Demonstrate several times how to turn the pages gently. Of course, books will be damaged. That is inevitable, especially with heavy-handed toddlers. Keep some books, particularly ones that have paper pages (as opposed to sturdy board pages), or movable parts out of reach and bring them out at special times during the day. Make certain children have books they can handle, that are stored on their eye level, and are easily accessible to them throughout the day. Include unusual books, such as wallpaper sample books (out-of-date copies donated by suppliers). Toddlers and twos can practice turning the sturdy pages while enjoying the interesting patterns.

Techniques for Reading to Infants

- At this age, reading should be a one-on-one experience, with the baby snuggled comfortably on your lap.
- Pick your time. Read when the child is rested and alert. A tired, hungry, or cranky baby will not enjoy the reading experience.
- Find a position that is comfortable for both of you. Place a young infant on your lap so her head is supported and hold the book within visual range, around 12" or so. Or lie on the floor next to the baby and hold the book above you so you can both see the picture comfortably.
- Read books the baby loves again and again. Certain books will become "old friends" as infants like familiar things.
- Encourage friends and family members to read to the baby. It is a great way to form a relationship with a baby, and the child learns that reading is something people do and enjoy together.

Techniques for Reading to Toddlers

- Anticipate reading with pleasure. "In a minute, when we finish putting these things away, we'll be able to read a book together."
- Set the stage. Get cozy. Snuggle into pillows or a big, soft chair.
- "Talk" the book rather than read it at first. Comment on the picture on each page. Do not skip pages, as this is confusing in the development of thought progression.
- Show your own interest. How you read can help toddlers listen more carefully, and support a sense of wonder and fascination.
- Don't rush. Take time to look at the pictures on each page. Respond to comments and be sensitive to the natural inquisitiveness that children may have about a particular image.
- Describe the process of reading as you do it. For example, look at the cover. Ask, "What do you think this book is about? Let's open it and see. Oh...look at this picture. What's that? What's she doing? Here is what these words say." Then point to the words as you read them. "Shall we turn the page and see what happens next?"

Read when the child is rested and alert. A tired, hungry, or cranky baby will not enjoy the reading experience.

Set the stage. Get cozy. Snuggle into pillows or a big, soft chair.

- Involve children in telling the story. When children are familiar with the book, let them tell you what will happen on the next page.
- Point out that you have reached the end of the story. End by saying something like: "And that's the end of the story. That was a nice story, wasn't it? I like this book. Do you like this book? Do you want to read it again?" This supports learning about the sequencing process (that stories have a beginning, middle, and end), which is important to children's total development.

Techniques for Reading to Two-Year-Olds
- Ask the children questions about the text. Help them reflect on the ideas.
- Connect the events to children's lives. "Is that how you felt when you had to come inside?"
- Encourage children to "read" books to you.
- Make the story fit. Elaborate, eliminate, or otherwise change your reading or telling of a story if it improves it for the children.
- "Tell" a book when it's not convenient to read it. Do the children recognize it?
- Have a small library corner with comfy pillows, good light, and a bookshelf.
- Ask the wonderful question, "Do you want to read it again?"

Techniques for Reading to a Mixed-Age Group
Reading to a mixed-age group of children who have different language abilities is still enjoyable for everyone.

- Don't force participation. Simply sit down with a book and see who shows up. Others may join you as the story continues.
- Simplify the text of a book, if necessary, so younger children can understand it.
- Let children take turns picking the book.
- Older children can enjoy books designed for younger children. They might add comments.
- Ask questions that extend ideas, such as, "What do you think he was thinking about in this picture?"
- When you read a book geared to the interests of older children, have other books there for younger ones to handle.

Easy Homemade Books
Homemade books can be "customized" for children using magazine pictures, photographs, or drawings. Here are a few simple ways to make books that are durable enough for young children to handle.

Encourage children to "read" books to you.

Don't force participation. Simply sit down with a book and see who shows up.

- Slip pictures into small photo albums with plastic sleeves or magnetic, clear pages.
- Sew sandwich-size, zip-closure plastic bags together along the bottom edge. Or, use clear vinyl tape to hold the bags together. Cut thin cardboard (such as file folders or poster board) to fit inside the bags. Put a picture on each side of the bag. Change the pictures in this book to keep it interesting.

- Mount pictures on construction paper trimmed to fit inside a small loose-leaf binder. Mark where the rings will be and punch holes. Stick reinforcers around the holes. Cover the front and back of each page with clear, self-adhesive paper and re-punch the holes. Insert in the loose-leaf binder.

WHITE GLUE

Add paper reinforcers to the holes

- Fold several sheets of construction paper in half. Glue pictures on each half and on the backs. Cover these sheets with clear, self-adhesive paper. Stack these covered sheets and sew with a sewing machine down the fold line.

Cover each sheet with clear adhesive paper

Making the Right Selections

There are important guidelines for selecting books that are most appropriate for each stage of development. Assessing book collections to be certain that they contain only the highest quality literature for children is an important and ongoing task. The selection tips included in the following sections are basic to most books used with very young children. In examining some of the classic picture books such as Ezra Jack Keats' *The Snowy Day*, Pat Kunhardt's *Pat the Bunny*, Eric Carle and Bill Martin Jr.'s *Brown Bear, Brown Bear, What Do You See?*, it becomes clear that a good picture book can be adapted to different interests and developmental stages. The familiarity and skill of the teacher or parent is the determining factor in the adaptability of any book. If a teacher feels comfortable telling the story from the pictures of a text-heavy book because the subject is dear to a two-year-old she or he is teaching, there is no reason the pictures can't be "read" to the two-year-old. In the end, teachers must use their judgment about the appropriateness of a book.

Books for Infants

Many of the following guidelines also apply to selecting books for toddlers and two-year-olds.

- Book topics should focus on things that are part of an infant's world. Stories with one picture on each page often have a theme that is carried throughout the book. For example, a book about "my day," with each picture related to activities that are common in an infant's day. The text in such stories is often only a word or two on each page, identifying the object on the page.
- Wordless books should be included in the book collections for all ages. They are particularly valuable for younger children because they learn to "read pictures" and match their spoken vocabulary with objects and illustrations in the stories.
- Illustrations or photographs should be realistic and easy for a child to comprehend.
- Bindings and inks should be durable and made of non-toxic materials.
- Stories should be simple, familiar concepts and limited to a few pages.
- Books of rhymes and chants should be part of everyday reading selections for infants.
- Some books in the collection should be small enough to be held easily by little hands. Small chunky board books or cloth books are excellent for the youngest children.

Stories should be about simple, familiar concepts and limited to a few pages.

Books for Toddlers and Twos

When selecting books for toddlers and twos, keep in mind that they are increasing their mobility every day and thus their world is becoming larger. Their interests will soon include friends, other people in the neighborhood, places they travel to with their families, and things they see and do on these adventures.

Important characteristics to remember when selecting books for toddlers and twos include:

- The story must capture children's interest in the first couple of pages.
- Illustrations or photographs must be of the highest quality and be clear and crisp, easy for a young child's eyes to decipher.
- Text and illustrations must work together on each page. The words must address the actions in the illustrations on that page.
- Text and illustrations must be free from stereotype or prejudice about any person or group of people.
- The story should stimulate the child's imagination.
- A sense of self-worth should be encouraged in the story.
- A wide range of family lifestyles and cultures should be represented in the book selections.
- Wordless books should be included in selections for toddlers and twos.
- Stories with minimal text and large print are best.
- Stories with repetitive phrases, rhyming language, and crisp dialogue will become favorites.
- Stories should celebrate independence and competency in children, and affirm the value of each child.

The Adult-Child-Book Triad of Interactions

Holding a child in your lap while you focus on a book together is a pleasurable experience for both child and adult. The talk centered on the book helps the child think with the adult about what she is seeing and hearing, and to process the language that is used. The three-month-old whose tiny hand is held by the teacher and "pats the furry bunny" is learning to interact with the picture and hear the sounds of the language while building the concept of bunnies as furry. When a six-month-old leans forward and pats the pictures several times, gurgling and cooing, we know that the child understands the language of the story and is already interacting

Illustrations or photographs must be of the highest quality and be clear and crisp, easy for a young child's eye to decipher.

Holding a child in your lap while you focus on a book together is a pleasurable experience for both child and adult.

with the book in appropriate ways. Language development and later literacy development are associated with these infant behaviors. They are forming pleasurable associations, are stimulated to talk about the book in the same way the adult does, and are showing signs that they understand that there is a sequence to the way one interacts with books. Providing a language-rich, print-rich, and literature-rich environment for young children ensures that children will have every opportunity to develop into good readers.

Interacting and Communicating with Books

The goal of reading to every child, every day can be difficult when the classroom is filled with infants, creepers, crawlers, toddlers, and twos. This type of reading challenges the teacher to interact with the book and remain attentive to the children. Helping infants to focus on the book, pointing out pictures, turning the pages, then helping them look at the next pictures can become a ritual. Try sitting in a rocking chair, holding the baby, and reading as you rock. It is not important that the baby look at the book all the time. Just hearing the language and the rhythm of reading aloud is reassuring, soothing, and enjoyable. After only a few sessions, infants may become more excited when the teacher approaches them with a book in hand.

Five- to seven-month-olds who are manipulating everything, even putting their feet in their mouths, are eager to manipulate the pages of books. Allow children to pat the pictures, bounce when they recognize a favorite scene, make noises while the teacher reads, and wiggle around. Encourage the movements and allow the children to redirect their attention, then refocus on the book and keep listening. Become attuned to the ebb and flow of the children's interest; do not push for attention or think that when the children aren't looking at the book that they have lost interest entirely. Given a moment's distraction, five- to seven-month-olds often return to focus on the book.

Youngsters who are creeping and crawling often pull up on an adult's legs to try to stand up. By this stage of development,

Providing a language-rich, print-rich, and literature-rich environment for young children ensures that children will have every opportunity to develop into good readers.

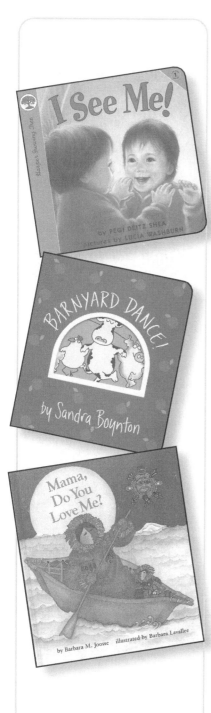

teachers have abandoned the rocking chair as the favorite place to read. Instead, they sit on the floor and begin reading to one child and are often joined by another child while the first one crawls away. As long as there is one child near, keep reading the book. If both children leave, wait for a moment or two, call attention to the book, and the children may crawl back again. Crawlers will begin to stay from the beginning to the end of the book. They will crawl into the teacher's lap, snuggle close while the book is read, and help to turn the pages. They often look in the teacher's face, pat the pages, and look down again expectantly as the page is turned. Some crawlers are book-babblers. While the teacher reads, they babble and attempt to match their babbling to the adult's reading. When they find a favorite page, they sometimes giggle, look up at the teacher, and wait for recognition that the adult remembers the significance of the picture. "Yes, I know you like this funny bear, don't you?"

Toddlers who walk around are also a challenge for a reading session. They are always on the move. Reading sessions can be described as a yo-yo. As the teacher reads, she or he holds the toddlers' attention for a while, and then the child moves a distance away. As the teacher reads more, the child comes back, goes out again, comes back more and more, and sometimes plops down onto the teacher's lap. This does not mean that they are not interested. If you stay in place and keep looking at the book, continuing to read, the children will return. Toddlers will begin spending longer and longer times on a teacher's lap or on the floor nearby. When a toddler sees a picture she likes, she may point with an index finger, look up to the teacher, smile, talk, giggle, or even repeat a phrase from the book. Toddlers love books about familiar things, such as a photograph album of pictures of the children playing in different areas of the room and on the playground.

Two-year-olds do not change dramatically from toddlers on their second birthdays. In fact, changes in specific behaviors characterized as belonging to two-year-olds can begin as early as 18 months. Conversely, two-year-olds often continue to behave like toddlers.

However, between ages 18 to 36 months, children grow much more literate. Even though children are filled with energy and need lots of large muscle activity, they are also developing the ability to "tell" their own stories, often embellishing events in a humorous way. Twos can move from being shy and retiring to wanting to be in the center of activity and to make things happen.

Reading to twos will help them make the sometimes difficult transition from dependence to independence. Reading to them will develop their ability to listen to stories with simple plots, which will enhance their love of books and reading. As their attention span increases, they will enjoy cumulative stories and stories with repetition. The s-t-r-e-t-c-h-e-r-s in this book offer children concrete activities, an essential experience for twos. Many of the suggested children's book-related experiences will help children develop new skills during this exciting time of growth.

Summary

Experienced caregivers, observant parents, and extensive research point to the same conclusion: Young children's language, cognitive, social, and emotional development is enhanced when caring adults interact with them with stories and pictures in books. This adult-child-book interaction helps children understand the way print appears on a page, how the pictures and illustrations are related to the content, how books provide ways of expressing feelings, and how stories unfold in a sequence with a beginning, middle, and a clear ending. Linking books with pleasurable activities in a child's life will expand a book's possibilities tremendously. We call these activities story s-t-r-e-t-c-h-e-r-s.

In the following chapters, we have selected wonderful children's books that are proven to be effective at capturing and holding the interests of infants, toddlers, and twos. Using the children's books as the basis, we recommend story s-t-r-e-t-c-h-e-r-s, or activities, to connect the content of the story with real-life experiences. Teachers' language interactions, selection of intriguing books, and the active story s-t-r-e-t-c-h-e-r-s help children develop their thinking abilities and build the concepts of print and print awareness that will help them become good readers and writers in later years.

Chapter 2—Books for Infants

Using Books with Infants

Everything is new for an infant! When you read to them often, and with pleasure, you create the possibility that books will be an important part of their world.

At first, infants benefit primarily from the sound of your voice and being close to you, feeling the warmth of your body as you cradle them close with the book in front of you, creating an important emotional connection with books. The child will soon associate books with the warm feeling of being in your arms and hearing your voice. You are shaping an attitude: "Reading feels good."

Infants also enjoy the visual images on the pages. You can see children's eyes widen and attention focus each time you turn the page and a new image appears. As you name the objects and talk about what is on the page, children hear the sounds and patterns of language. Later they will learn that objects are connected to certain sounds or words.

Infants enjoy books with pictures of familiar objects, and books with a strong rhythmic quality and rich language sounds.

Infants have an instinctive interest in faces, especially the faces of children and other babies. They focus on the eyes, and they seem to comprehend facial expressions. For this reason, many books for infants are illustrated with large, interesting faces for them to enjoy. They also enjoy books with pictures of familiar objects, and books with a strong rhythmic quality and rich language sounds. When infants start to babble, they are playing with the sounds and rhythms of language. Focus on these aspects as you read books.

As babies become more active and are able to scootch or crawl around and can pick things up, they develop *object hunger*, an intense interest in objects. They are slowly gaining control of their hand muscles and want to practice many different hand movements such as picking things up, feeling things with their fingertips, poking their fingers in holes, releasing (dropping) things, and throwing things. There is an innate drive to examine and mouth every object they encounter. They are finding out about their world and the relationship of spaces and shapes as

well as properties of objects—hardness, softness, what round things do, and so on. Books like *Pat the Bunny* by Dorothy Kunhardt have "things to do" embedded in the book—textures to feel, flaps to lift, tabs to pull, interesting holes and shapes. It's best not to leave these books out for free exploration, because children may unintentionally destroy them. Instead, let children enjoy this kind of book while sitting in your lap.

Toward the end of the first year children discover that things still exist even though they cannot be seen. This is called *object permanence.* While infants are learning about object permanence, they invent simple games of peekaboo, covering things up and uncovering them again, dropping things into containers and dumping them out again, and crawling behind furniture. A book, when you think about it, is actually a "peekaboo" system—each page uncovers a new image.

Over time, as you read books again and again, children learn how a book "works." They discover that there will be a new image and new sounds of language each time a page is turned. When you read to infants, they are learning to *attend*—to pay attention to one thing and screen out other things in the room. As the reader, you are also focusing on the same thing, talking about the image on the page. This is a critical skill for later learning.

Techniques for Reading to Infants
- At this age, reading should be a one-on-one experience, with the baby snuggled comfortably on your lap.
- Pick your time. Read when the child is rested and alert. A tired, hungry, or cranky baby will not enjoy the reading experience.
- Find a position that is comfortable for both of you. Place a young infant on your lap so her head is supported and hold the book within visual range, around 12" or so. Or lie on the floor next to the baby and hold the book above you so you can both see the picture comfortably.
- Read books the baby loves again and again. Certain books will become "old friends" as infants like familiar things.
- Encourage friends and family members to read to the baby. It is a great way to form a relationship with a baby, and the child learns that reading is something people do and enjoy together.

Read books children love again and again.

Remember, you don't always need to "stretch" the story with follow-up activities. Feel free to enjoy the books just as a reading experience. S-t-r-e-t-c-h-e-r-s are especially good to do once the child is familiar with the book. The activities in this section are, of necessity, very simple. All of these books can be used with older children, so you can add complexity to the s-t-r-e-t-c-h-e-r-s as the child grows.

Feel free to enjoy books just as a reading experience.

Books and S-t-r-e-t-c-h-e-r-s

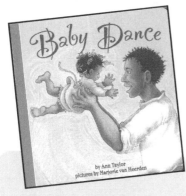

Baby Dance

by Ann Taylor, illustrated by Marjorie van Heerden

Story Synopsis

A tired mommy falls asleep on the couch. In order to give the mother a little rest, the daddy plays with the baby in an exuberant dance. Vibrant illustrations reflect the joy of the interactions between father and baby.

Reading Hints

Modulate your voice as you read the book. Accent the rhyming words once you have the text memorized. For extra fun, dance with the baby while you tell the story.

Story S-t-r-e-t-c-h-e-r: Language

Whisper

Materials

no special materials needed

- Just as the father and baby in the book had a hard time keeping quiet, it can be difficult for all young children to learn to moderate their voice and actions.
- If the baby talks or makes sounds, see if he can imitate you whispering and "shushing" to be very quiet.

Do the Baby Dance

Materials
no special materials needed

- Pick up a baby and do a dance similar to that shown in the book.
- Make sure the baby wants to do this and is having fun.
- Slow down if his face shows anxiety. The point is to enjoy the interaction.

Dance with Dolly

Materials
doll or stuffed animal

- Encourage a child or children to help a doll or stuffed animal "dance."

Pick up a baby and do a dance.

Something to Think About

Fathers typically play with babies with a different style than mothers. They are much more active, often swinging and tossing the child. It is important that the child has good head, neck, and torso control before such active play is initiated. Be sure to watch the baby's face carefully for cues that indicate fear or discomfort. Some people are unaware of the dangers that can result from overactive play with babies. During pre-service, or at least once a year, train all staff and volunteers about this issue. Ask a nurse to talk to the staff about Shaken Baby Syndrome.

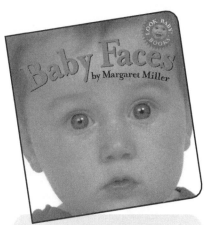

Baby Faces
by Margaret Miller

Story Synopsis
Large, close-up photographs depict faces of babies showing a range of expressions on each right-hand page. One word that describes the expression on the baby's face appears on each left-hand page.

Reading Hints
As you read each page, look at the child and make the face that appears on the pictured face. The child will probably imitate the expression.

Story S-t-r-e-t-c-h-e-r: Language

Make a Face to Match the Word

Materials
no special materials needed

- Read this book many times so the children are familiar with it.
- Each time encourage the child or children to make the faces in the book.
- After the children have "practiced" the faces many times, say one of the words. See if they can come up with the corresponding face without looking at the book.

Magazine Faces

Materials

old magazines

scissors (adult use only)

cardboard or construction paper

glue

clear contact paper or laminating paper

- Let one or two children help you find pictures of children's faces in magazines.
- Cut them out and glue them to the cardboard or construction paper.
- Laminate or cover with clear contact paper for durability.
- Look through these face pictures with the children and make up words to go with them.

Reflected Emotions

Materials

unbreakable mirror

- Let the child enjoy making faces in the mirror. Play along!
- While the child is making faces in the mirror, name the emotion on his face. "Happy" or "sad" are usually the first faces young children recognize.
- If they make faces that express other emotions, name these emotions.

Something to Think About

Babies learn to "read" facial expressions very early in life, long before the words to describe them are mastered. It is very important that babies see lots of smiles and happy, pleasant people whose faces mirror those emotions.

Bathtime, Colors, and Playtime,

DK Soft Books
by Dorling Kindersley

Story Synopsis

These vinyl-covered foam rubber books must be squeezed! Each has bright, beautiful illustrations with single word labels. On the left-hand page Bathtime describes the steps in taking a bath, and the right-hand pages have one-word labels of items associated with that step. Colors focuses on one color for each two-page spread. Playtime describes play situations, such as playing outside, playing together, or playing on the beach on the left-hand pages and the right-hand pages have one-word labels of items associated with that type of play.

Reading Hints

These books are designed for infants to handle and mouth. Even if thrown, they will not hurt anyone. While the children will enjoy having an adult read one of these books, they can also enjoy them independently.

Story S-t-r-e-t-c-h-e-r: Language

Color Collection

Materials

brightly colored objects with one dominant color the same as the colors on the pages of the *Colors* book

- Group like-colored objects together.
- Let the child play with them.
- As you read the book with the child, pick up objects of the same color as those on the page you are looking at.
- Name the color and talk about it with the child.

Toy/Picture Match

Materials

toys that match those in the *Playtime* book

- Gather a few of the toys pictured in the *Playtime* book.
- Put the toys in your lap.
- As you read the book with the child, point to a picture of a toy that is in your lap.
- One by one, pick up the toys from your lap and ask the child if the toy you are holding is like the one in the book.

Bathtime Fun

Materials

objects that are the same or similar to objects
  in the *Bathtime* book

- After reading the book together, place a few of the items from the book (such as a small towel, a bath sponge, a rubber duck) in front of the child.
- Encourage him to touch the objects.
- Show him the pictures of these objects in the book.
- Let him play with the bathtime objects.

Something to Think About

Infants are not going to learn the names of colors from these activities. However, grouping various objects of the same strong color may plant the seed of awareness and understanding of the concept.

Country Animals, Farm Animals, Garden Animals, and Pet Animals

Board Books
by Lucy Cousins

Story Synopsis

These four small board books are the essence of simplicity. Uncomplicated illustrations on a single color background, one per page or double page spread, depict common animals. The only words in the book are labels for the animals.

Reading Hints

Young infants will enjoy touching each animal as you name it. Older infants will enjoy trying to say the name of the animal. These books are perfect for opening to any page and naming the animal.

Story S-t-r-e-t-c-h-e-r: Language

Animal Sounds

Materials
no special materials are needed

- Make a sound for the animal on each page.
- Wait for the child to imitate you.
- Once the child is able to repeat the sound a few times, he might make the sound of the animal after you name it.

Animal Pictures

Materials
pictures of animals cut from magazines
cardboard
glue
clear contact paper or laminating film
shoebox

- Mount individual pictures of animals on cardboard.
- Laminate or cover with clear contact paper for durability.
- Let the children handle the pictures and carry them around as they walk.
- As you read the books, look at other pictures of the same animals you see on the pages.
- Keep these pictures and the books in a small box, such as a shoebox.

Toy Animals

Materials
toy animals of any type that are safe to have around babies, such as stuffed animals, or toy animals made of rubber, wood, or plastic

- Let the child play with the toy animals. Name the animal the child is playing with.
- Help the child find the matching animal to the one pictured. "Walk" the toy animal up to the page and touch it to the page.
- You might make a noise, or say something like, "Hi, Dog!"

Something to Think About

These books will be more meaningful to a child who has seen real animals that are pictured in the books. However, even if the children have not seen the animals, they will learn to recognize the animals' attributes.

Do You Know New?

by Jean Marzollo, illustrated by Mari Takabayashi

Story Synopsis

The rhyming text on these pages emphasizes the "oo" sound. The book has clear, bright illustrations featuring children's faces. The last page is a reflective surface, which lets the baby see his own image.

Reading Hints

New, do, you, two, shoe, moo and other "oo" sounds are used in this rhyming story. As you read the story, emphasize the "oo" sounds. When babies start to coo and babble, the "oo" sound is often among the first sounds they make. Always respond to babies' early communication with similar sounds.

Story S-t-r-e-t-c-h-e-r: Language

Conversation of Coos

Materials
clean blanket

- Place a baby on his back on the floor on a clean blanket.
- Lean over the baby.
- When he makes a sound, imitate it as exactly as you can, making eye contact.
- See if the child answers you with eye contact and another sound. See how long you can keep this "conversation" going.

Story S-t-r-e-t-c-h-e-r: Language

Chanting

Materials
no special materials needed

- Babies will often chant singsong syllables and sounds. Reinforce this valuable language practice by imitating the child's chants.
- Initiate this chanting, using sounds and nonsense syllables in different intonations.

Baby in the Mirror

Materials
unbreakable mirror

- After discovering the reflected image on the last page, take the child to see his reflection in other mirrors in the room.
- Wave to the baby in the mirror.
- Say, "Hi baby!"
- A young infant does not yet realize that the reflection is himself and may try to pat the baby in the mirror.

Something to Think About

This is a good book for a very young baby because babies like the "ooooooo" sound. It is one of the first sounds a baby can imitate.

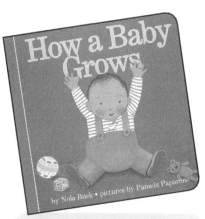

How a Baby Grows

by Nola Buck, illustrated by Pamela Paparone

Story Synopsis

The familiar world of the infant is portrayed in a rhyming text and simple, easy-to-recognize illustrations. The child will eventually enjoy pointing to and later naming the objects in the illustrations. Children of different races are well represented.

Reading Hints

This active story talks about things a baby sees, needs, speaks, hears, and shares. Many of the events in the story will be familiar to the children. Showing the children the real life events portrayed in the book will connect the story with the children's everyday life.

Story S-t-r-e-t-c-h-e-r: Language

Where's the Bunny?

Materials

no special materials needed

■ As you read the book to the children, challenge them to find something on each page. "Where's the bunny? Where's the bottle?"

■ Smiles and positive responses to a child as he touches the picture when you ask a questions will reinforce his learning and enjoyment.

Can You Find _____?

Materials

objects that are the same as or similar to things pictured in the
book, such as an unbreakable baby bottle, a rattle,
a toy duck, a ball, and a teddy bear

- Place the objects on the floor in front of the children.
- Let the children play with the objects.
- As you read the book, see if the children can find some of the
  real objects represented in the illustrations.

What Does Your Baby Need?

Materials

dolls and doll props, such as a high chair, doll bottle, diaper

- Once children are familiar with the book, ask, "Let's play with
  your baby. Does she need a diaper now? Is she wet? Is he
  hungry? Does he need a bottle?"
- Help the children play with the dolls by holding them and
  gently rocking and singing to the dolls.

Something to Think About

Children learn the skills of pretend play from a participating adult or an older child. This kind of play has many learning purposes as the child develops, and it's an enjoyable way to interact. Touching objects or things that you are talking about helps the baby associate the word with the object.

I See Me!

by Pegi Deitz Shea, illustrated by Lucia Washburn

Story Synopsis

Realistic illustrations and descriptive text depict a baby's fascination in finding her face reflected in a mirror, a spoon, a television screen, pots and pans, a shiny faucet, sunglasses, and a window pane. These "ah ha" moments of discovery are invaluable to a baby's growth.

Reading Hints

Let the child find the "other baby" in the reflective surface of each illustration.

Story S-t-r-e-t-c-h-e-r: Object Play

Shiny Toys

Materials

safe objects with shiny surfaces, such as pots and pot lids or large metal spoons, or any other shiny object that will not break

■ Let the child play with these objects, finding his own reflection.

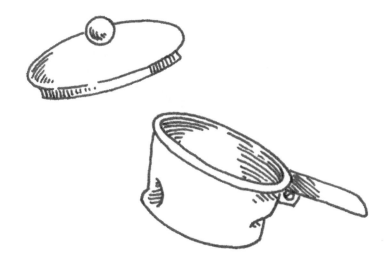

Hats

Materials
different hats
unbreakable mirror

- Put a hat on one of the children.
- Let him look in the mirror while he is wearing the hat.
- Put a hat on another child.
- Let the children play with the hats independently.

Where Is Your Face?

Materials
various reflective surfaces in the environment

- Carry a baby around the environment and help him find his reflection in various surfaces. All of the surfaces in the book are easy to find in most child care centers.
- Say, "Hi," and wave to the baby in the reflection.

Something to Think About

Babies love faces, especially of other babies. This book gives them faces to admire, and will encourage them to enjoy their own face when they see it reflected. Check the bibliography (pages 217-219) for other titles that feature babies' faces.

The Itsy-Bitsy Spider

by Rosemary Wells

Story Synopsis

Rosemary Wells illustrates this classic children's rhyme with a curious duck that has delightful facial expressions. Learning about rain and sunshine and wet and dry are added benefits of the enjoyable, musical rhyme.

Reading Hints

It's almost impossible to read this book without singing it! If you sing the story, be sure to sing the part of the rhyme that matches the illustration on the open page of the book.

Story S-t-r-e-t-c-h-e-r: Movement

Hand Rhyme

Materials

no special materials needed

■ Demonstrate the hand motions that go with the poem.
■ Help the child move his hands as you sing the rhyme.

Story S-t-r-e-t-c-h-e-r: Movement

What Can You Do with Your Hands?

Materials

no special materials needed

- Help the child explore all the different ways to move his hands.
- Demonstrate motions to imitate, such as clapping, waving, "walking" fingers, and so on.

Story S-t-r-e-t-c-h-e-r: Sensory

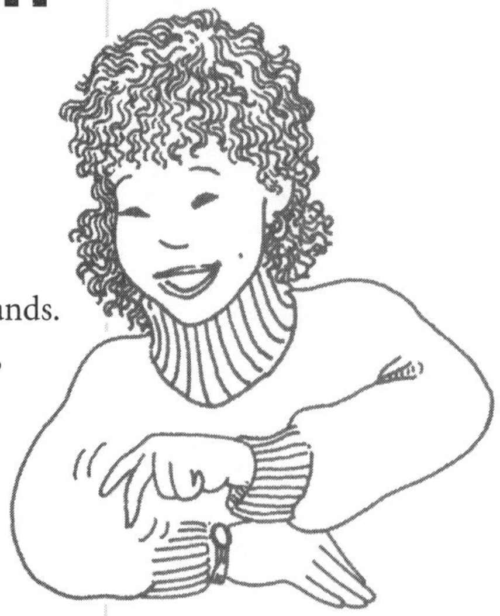

Watch the Rain

Materials

a rainy day

- If you have a covered area outside, take the children there.
- Talk to them about what is happening to the bugs, flowers, grass, walkway, trees, and other things that they can see.
- Talk about the wonderful rain and all the good things it does.
- If you do not have a covered area, sit by a window with one or two children and watch the rain.
- Sometimes it's nice to watch the rain and just listen to the sounds the rain makes.

Something to Think About

The more senses involved in an activity, the easier it is to remember. That is the basic reason behind all the "hand rhymes." Children like to move their hands while you recite poetry. When they watch the rain, they can move their fingers up and down like the rain.

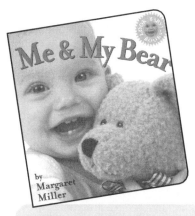

Me & My Bear
by Margaret Miller

Story Synopsis

This board book has a different baby on each page, and each baby has its own special bear. The simple text describes the special characteristic of each bear and what the baby and the bear are doing.

Reading Hints

Let a baby bring a special bear to sit with him while you read this story. Read slowly, allowing time for the babies to consider thoughtfully what each bear and baby are doing. As a baby's understanding grows more sophisticated, he will want to help his bear do what the bears in the story are doing.

Story S-t-r-e-t-c-h-e-r: Object Play

Bear Collection

Materials

stuffed bears

- Gather all the bears (or other stuffed animals) in one space and allow the child to play with them.
- While he plays, comment on the different characteristics of each bear. "This one is for hugging." "This bear wants to do a somersault."

Our Special Bears

Materials

children's special bears

camera

- Allow each child to have a special bear with him.
- Talk about each child's bear, noticing its characteristics.
- At naptime, tuck the bear in with the child, and sing a lullaby to the bear.
- Take a photograph of each child with his special bear.
- Display these photographs where the children can see them and talk about them often.
- Make two copies of each photograph so one can be sent home. Encourage the parents to display the photograph at their child's eye level so he can see it.

Soft and Not Soft

Materials

collection of stuffed animals

other toys that are not soft, such as toy trucks, rattles and books

- Talk about how nice it is to squeeze and hug the soft toys.
- Notice that it is not as pleasant to squeeze hard toys.
- Help the child sort the toys into two piles, soft toys in one, hard toys in the other.

Take a photograph of each child with his special bear.

Something to Think About

Every child needs a teddy bear or some soft, sympathetic stuffed animal. When the child experiences "stranger anxiety," which usually begins at about 10 months, it can be very comforting to have a bear friend at one's side. This is one toy a child should not be expected to share.

My Friends
by Nancy Tafuri

Story Synopsis

Baby animals are beautifully illustrated in this board book, with one animal on each page. The name of the animal is written underneath its picture. The baby in the story is reading about his animal friends. On the last page he points out that all of them are babies just like him.

Reading Hints

Let the child spend time with the baby animal on each page. It is fun to talk about the different sounds each baby animal makes.

Story S-t-r-e-t-c-h-e-r: Language

Visit Real Animals

Materials

petting zoo, small farm, or owner of a baby animal

- Find a place in your community that has a variety of real animals, such as a petting zoo or small farm. Or, invite someone with a baby animal to bring it to visit you.
- Letting the children see and, with guidance, touch the baby animal will give the children a deeper understanding of animals, which will be reinforced by the pictures in the book.

Magazine Picture Match

Materials
old magazines
scissors (adult use only)
construction paper or cardboard
glue
clear contact paper or laminating
    material

- Find magazine pictures that
  correspond to the animals pictured in
  the book.
- Cut them out, glue them to the construction paper
  or cardboard, and laminate them or cover them
  with clear contact paper.
- Help a child find pictures of animals that correspond
  to those illustrated in the book.
- Notice similarities and differences. This will help broaden the
  child's understanding of what a kitten or any other baby
  animal can look like.

Be an Animal

Materials
no special materials needed

- Show the child how to make noises and movements that
  imitate the animals pictured.
- The child will eventually use the picture as a cue to imitate the
  animal.

Something to Think About

Very young children are fascinated by animals, especially baby animals with large eyes. This is an ideal time to model gentleness and kindness toward animals. There is no particular age at which children begin to make sounds like animals and imitate the movements of animals. Each child develops at his own pace, and when he is ready, he will do it. However, even before he is able to do these things, he will enjoy listening and seeing others do them.

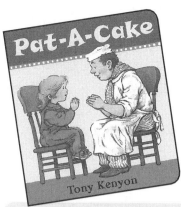

Pat-a-Cake
by Tony Kenyon

Story Synopsis
This board book illustrates the words of the traditional baby lap game and adds a humorous ending. This is also a very nice sibling story. The illustrations tell the story of a young child asking the baker for a cake to share with her baby sister.

Reading Hints
As you read this book with a child next to you, demonstrate the actions. Read it through again and move the child's hands. Be sure to notice the expressions on the faces of the baker and child in the book. Read the book with the appropriate expression in your voice.

Story S-t-r-e-t-c-h-e-r: Pretending

Play Pat-a-Cake with a Doll

Materials
doll or stuffed animal

- Help the doll do the motions of pat-a-cake while saying the words.
- Then hand the doll to a child and say, "Now you do it."
- Chant the rhyme and let him help the doll make the motions.

Make a Cookie Cake

Materials

roll of plain sugar cookie dough (or make your own
cookie dough)
pan for baking cookies
oven (requires careful supervision)

- Read the story and talk with children about the baker and what he is doing.
- Take a piece of cookie dough and let a child "poke" and "pat" it on the cookie sheet. Mark this "cookie cake" with his initials.
- Repeat with each child.
- While the cookies are baking, say the rhyme and make the actions with the children.
- When baked and cooled, eat the cookie cakes with the children.

Note: Closely supervise the children when baking the cookies and the oven is hot. In addition, be sure that you have parents' permission for the children to eat cookies.

Playdough Cakes

Materials

playdough

- Encourage the child to poke, pound, and roll the playdough while you chant the rhyme from the book.

Something to Think About

This traditional game is excellent for building social ties between children and adults or older children. This game teaches infants that it is fun to be with other people.

Pat the Bunny
by Dorothy Kunhardt

Story Synopsis

This classic "touch and feel" book gives an infant something to do each time the page turns. Capitalizing on an infant's natural learning style of imitation, the illustrations of the children, Judy or Paul, on the left side of each page show the child what to do on the right side of the page, such as patting a bunny, playing peekaboo, and reading a book.

Reading Hints

Even though this book is made of strong materials, it can be damaged by rough usage. For that reason, it is best offered as a lap book. With a child comfortably seated on your lap, encourage him to touch the pages and enjoy the textures and simple hand manipulations the book invites.

Story S-t-r-e-t-c-h-e-r: Object Play

Peekaboo with You

Materials
scarf or towel

- After reading the "Judy can play peekaboo with Paul" page, drape the scarf or towel over your head and encourage a child to pull it off (or you pull it off) as you say, "Peekaboo!"
- Repeat as often as it is fun for the baby.

Texture Book

Materials
textured materials such as terrycloth, felt, sandpaper, and fake fur
glue
thin cardboard or index cards to fit the size of binder
hole punch
small loose-leaf binder

■ Glue a different textured material onto the thin cardboard or index cards.

■ Punch holes on left side of the cardboard or index cards and insert them into the loose-leaf binder.

■ Allow the child to turn the pages and feel the textures on the pages.

Find Your Reflection

Materials
common shiny objects such as an unbreakable mirror, a
    doorknob, or a pot lid

■ When you read the "Judy can look in the mirror" page, help the child look at his reflection in such things as an unbreakable mirror, shiny pots, a doorknob, or other shiny objects in your environment.

Something to Think About

Infants are eager to use all of their senses in every way possible. Provide an on-going variety of interesting things to touch, see, hear, and smell. (They will put any object in their mouth, providing a taste experience whether you plan it or not, so make sure things are safe and non-toxic.)

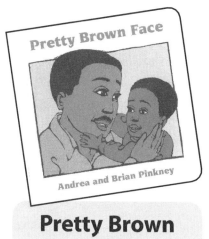

Pretty Brown Face

Andrea and Brian Pinkney

Pretty Brown Face

by Andrea and Brian Pinkney

Story Synopsis

This rhyming book features a father and his baby admiring the beautiful face in the mirror. The end of the book offers a mirrored surface so the child can admire his own face.

Reading Hints

When a child admires his face on the mirrored back page, touch his features and name and describe them. If you are reading to a small group of children, show each child the pretty face in the mirror on the back page.

Story S-t-r-e-t-c-h-e-r: Sensory

Mirror Fun

Materials
non-toxic tempera paint
unbreakable hand mirror

- Before a child looks in the mirror, put a dot of non-toxic tempera paint (or any other substance that is easy to wipe off) on his nose.
- Let the child hold the hand mirror and see his face.
- Point to and name the child's features while the child is looking in the mirror, "just like the little boy in the book."
- See if he notices the dot of paint in the reflection in the mirror and tries to remove it from his own nose.

Peekaboo Mirror

Materials
unbreakable wall mirror at child's eye level
curtain rod and curtain

- Hang a curtain over the mirror.
- Show the child how to pull the curtain aside and say, "Peekaboo, (child's name)!"

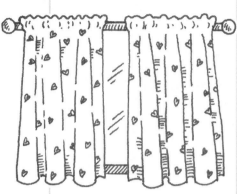

All Kinds of Hair

Materials
dolls with different kinds of hair

- When you read the page about hair, touch the child's hair, then let the child touch your hair.
- Talk about how it feels.
- Find dolls with different kinds of hair and let the child feel them.
- When appropriate, ask other people if the child can touch their hair.
- Comment on how it feels, always in admiring ways.

Something to Think About

All children need to see images of children who look like them. Indeed, it is important for all children to see respectful and attractive representations of people of all races so they are comfortable in a diverse society.

Ring the Bells!, Shake the Maracas!, Tap the Tambourine!

Rockin' Rhythm Band Board Books by Billy Davis

Story Synopsis

These books have built-in musical instruments that will delight any infant. Tap the Tambourine! has words and illustrations for "Old MacDonald Had a Farm," Shake the Maracas!, "Row, Row, Row Your Boat," and Ring the Bells!, "Twinkle, Twinkle, Little Star."

Reading Hints

It's almost impossible to read these books without singing them. So let yourself sing! Of course, you can't read a book and look at the pictures if you are shaking the book at the same time, so instead, let a child tap the book to make the instrument produce its sound.

Story S-t-r-e-t-c-h-e-r: Music

Paper Towel Tube Band

Materials

paper towel tubes, two per child
recorded music

■ Let the child tap the paper towel tubes together while lively music is playing. (Or use them while singing one of the songs from the books.)
■ Comment on the nice, hollow sound they make.

Note: It's best to put these away again after this activity because children might smash them in their play, and then they won't make a nice sound anymore.

Story S-t-r-e-t-c-h-e-r: Object Play

Shake, Shake Bottles

Materials

plastic bottles
objects to place inside individual bottles, such as buttons or jingle bells
super glue (adult use only)
strong clear tape

- Put some of the loose materials inside the bottles.
- Glue the caps on securely. Cover with strong tape.
- Let the child shake the bottles to make the different sounds.
- Sing one of the songs while he shakes them.

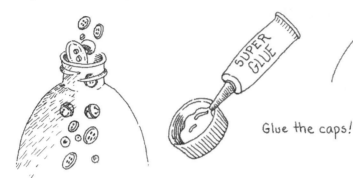

Glue the caps!

Secure the caps with tape!

Cellophane Squeeze

Materials
old, clean pantyhose
scissors (adult use only)
cellophane (adult handling only)

- Cut off a section of a pantyhose or nylon stocking leg.
- Tie a knot in one end.
- Stuff some crinkly cellophane into it, and tie a knot at the other end. This encases the cellophane, making it safe. Because pieces can tear off and infants can choke on it, cellophane should not be given to young children to play with without a protective covering.
- Let a child squeeze and pat the nylon stocking-encased cellophane to make an interesting sound.

stuff with crinkly cellophane

CRINKLE!

CRINKLE!

Something to Think About

Infants love toys that make something happen. One of the joyful discoveries of the infant year is the different ways to make noise. These books have that extra appeal. While they are learning these three "first songs of childhood" with you, the instruments help them feel the rhythm of language as well.

Scratch and Sniff: Food; Scratch and Sniff: Garden; Scratch and Sniff: Party; and Scratch and Sniff: Shopping

Scratch and Sniff Board Books by Dorling Kindersley

Story Synopsis

This series of four books may be as appealing to adults as to children. Vivid color photographs accompany remarkably recognizable scents. **Scratch and Sniff: Garden** *presents photos and fragrances of roses, lavender, mint, cedar, and freshly cut grass. Use* **Scratch and Sniff: Shopping** *to experience ginger cookies, new shoes, flowers, an apple, and perfume.* **Scratch and Sniff: Food** *offers bananas, pizza, oranges, chocolate, and strawberries. Birthday cake, pineapple, cola, fruit-scented bubbles, and mint candies are represented in* **Scratch and Sniff: Party.**

Reading Hints

These books smell so good the children may want to lick and taste the pictures! You will have to show the child how to scratch the picture on the right hand page and then put it up to his nose to smell. You might need to demonstrate how to sniff.

Story S-t-r-e-t-c-h-e-r: Sensory

Things to Smell

Materials

objects with strong fragrances, including some of the things represented in the books, such as a piece of cedar, a banana, leather shoes, or an apple

■ Invite the child to smell one of the objects, and then, if appropriate, to smell the same object in the book.
■ Ask an older infant, "Do they smell the same?"
■ Try this with another object.

Take a Smell Walk

Materials

no special materials are needed

- Read *Scratch and Sniff: Garden.*
- Take a walk and see how many interesting things you can find to smell.
- Hold a child or seat him where he can see and smell the things you find.

Banana Tasting Party

Materials

ripe bananas

plate

kitchen knife (adult use only)

paper towels

damp cloths

hand-washing supplies

- This activity is for older infants who are eating solid foods.
- Cut up a banana into pieces that fit into small hands. Set aside.
- Read *Scratch and Sniff: Food.*
- Encourage the child to smell the banana before he eats it.
- Talk about how it feels, how it smells, and how it tastes.

Note: Before doing this activity or any other activity with food, check with parents to be sure that the babies have eaten bananas before and that you have their permission to serve them to the children.

Something to Think About

Infants are rarely conscious of their sense of smell and don't really know how to sniff and smell an object. These books will help them become more aware of the function of their nose. They may find added pleasure in using this sense.

Show Me!

by Tom Tracy, illustrated by Darcia Labrosse

Story Synopsis

A mother and her baby are playing a wonderful game where the mother admires the baby's nose, cheek, chin, tummy, toes, and arms. The book shows this mother and baby enjoying this affectionate rhyming game.

Reading Hints

When the story is read to one baby at a time, it is fun to do some of the games that are being played in the book with the baby.

Story S-t-r-e-t-c-h-e-r: Language

Show Me Your Nose

Materials
no special materials needed

- Name various body parts for the child to point to. The body parts in the story are cheek, nose, chin, tummy, knees, toes, and arms.
- Each time you read the story, add a new body part and show the child where it is mentioned in the book.

Clapping Game

Materials

no special materials needed

- After you have read the story several times over a period of days and the children are more aware of the parts of their bodies, play this clapping game.
- Make up a tune and show the children how to clap as you sing. For example, sing "Old MacDonald Had a Farm" and clap your hands.
- When the children know how to clap their hands to the song, try clapping your arms or your legs. Clap only one part of the body at a time.

Do It to the Doll

Materials

doll or stuffed animal

- When children are very familiar with the book and have enjoyed the motions and interactions, encourage one to "tweak the cheek" or "wiggle the chin" of a doll or stuffed animal while you read the story.
- Imitating the actions in the book will help children learn the meaning of the words.

Make up a tune and show the children how to clap as you sing.

Something to Think About

Pretend play is a way to try out real-life scenarios, the things children see the adults in their lives doing. It is very important to model the kind of behavior we want children to imitate. Imitation is a powerful way for children to learn.

Spot Goes to the Park, Spot's Touch and Feel Day, and Where's Spot?

by Eric Hill

Story Synopsis

*In **Where's Spot?**, Sally, the mother dog, searches all over the house for Spot, lifting all kinds of doors and lids where he might be. She finally finds him in his basket. This and the other Spot books give children many opportunities to lift a flap and discover surprises underneath.*

Reading Hints

All of these books are "sit on a lap and read with an adult" books. The many flaps that form the framework of the stories can be easily torn or ripped off accidentally by the child's heavy touch—a good reason to keep these books "special."

Story S-t-r-e-t-c-h-e-r: Language

Covered Pictures

Materials
pictures cut from magazines
cardboard
scissors (adult use only)
glue
duct tape
fabric

- Mount pictures on cardboard.
- Cut a piece of fabric to match the size of the picture.
- Use duct tape to attach the fabric to the top of the picture.
- Children enjoy lifting the flap to see the picture underneath.
- Make these available for the children to handle and carry around, or hang them at the children's eye level on a wall or the back of a shelf.

Friends under Flaps

Materials

2 pieces of poster board

photographs of the child's friends, family members, and pets

glue

Exacto knife (adult use only)

wide tape

- Glue photographs to one piece of poster board.
- Place the second piece of poster board on top and mark where the photographs are.
- Remove the second piece of poster board and use the Exacto knife to cut little doors (rectangles with 3 sides cut) where the photographs were.
- Place the poster board with the doors cut in it over the poster board with the photographs glued on.
- Tape these two pieces of poster board together around the edges.
- Attach this to the wall or the back of a shelf.
- Children can open the doors to find and name their friends.

Glue photos to one piece of poster board

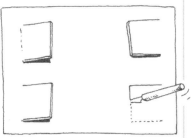

Cut doors on second piece of board

Place second piece on top of first

Containers with Lids

Materials

collection of boxes and containers that have attached lids, such as cigar boxes, diaper wipes boxes, and plastic storage boxes

small toys and stuffed animals

- Let the children play with the boxes.
- They will love putting the toys inside and closing the lid.
- Leave surprises inside the boxes from time to time.

Something to Think About

Young children find containers with lids and things behind hinged doors irresistible. Kitchen cabinets, lidded baskets, and the like give them practice at their favorite game of peekaboo, making something appear and disappear again. Be sure that all the objects are large enough that they do not pose a choking hazard.

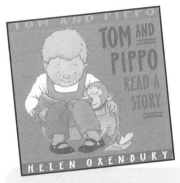

Tom and Pippo Read a Story

by Helen Oxenbury

Story Synopsis

The story line of this book is a familiar one: the eager child, Tom, brings book after book to the father who would rather be reading his newspaper. When the father is finished reading to Tom, the clever child figures out a way to get another story. He says his monkey, Pippo, wants a story.

Reading Hints

This book would be fun to read with a child's favorite stuffed animal or special toy tucked closely in at your side. Notice what the cat is doing on each page.

Story S-t-r-e-t-c-h-e-r: Language

Story Time at the Library

Materials
local library

■ This is a great time to introduce children to story time for little ones at the local library.

■ Arrange a field trip to your local library. (Bring additional staff or parent volunteers.)

■ Sit with the children to enjoy the librarian's story and the company of other children.

Book Nook

Materials

small bookshelf
cushions
stuffed animals
hanging lamp (optional)

- As you read the book, notice that Tom has his books scattered on the floor. Say, "He needs a book nook. So do we!"
- Arrange a cozy area with a small bookshelf, pillows, cushions, and good lighting.
- Let the children help you place the books on the shelf and comment on how nice it looks.
- Read one or two books to try it out.

Read to Teddy

Materials

teddy bear or another favorite doll or stuffed animal

- After reading the book, say, "Tom read the book to Pippo. What a good idea! I bet you and I could read this book to Teddy (or whatever the child has named the toy)."
- Help the child place the teddy next to him in your lap and read the book again. Afterward talk about how much teddy enjoyed sitting down and listening to the story.
- When the child is ready, he will "read" to teddy on his own.

Something to Think About

When a child reads to a doll or stuffed animal, he is demonstrating certain understandings about books—that both reader and listener must see the book, that you turn the pages, that you make sounds for each page, and so on. Notice how much book-reading behavior the child learns as he grows into the toddler stage.

Touch and Feel: Clothes; Touch and Feel: Home; Touch and Feel: Kitten; and Touch and Feel: Puppy

Touch and Feel Books by Dorling Kindersley

Story Synopsis

This series of sturdy board books gives infants many irresistible textures to touch, embedded in clear, bright photographs of familiar objects. The bold print in the text emphasizes the descriptive words, coaching the reader to be especially expressive. The cover of each book has a cutout, exposing a tantalizing texture underneath and inviting the child's interest in the book.

Reading Hints

The visual and tactile images of these books are so beautiful that children will be eager to turn the pages back and forth. Since there is no necessary sequence to the text, enjoy the books in any order.

Story S-t-r-e-t-c-h-e-r: Language

Which One Is It?

Materials

real objects of the pictures in any of the books, such as a teddy bear, a laundry basket, a mirror, and a terrycloth towel

- Let the child play with the objects and then touch the pictures in the book.
- Gather several of the objects around you.
- Point to a picture in the book and ask the child, "Which is the *fluffy* teddy bear?" (or the pictured object you point to).
- See if he can pick out or point to the correct object.

Puppies and Kittens

Materials
stuffed dog, cat, puppy, or kitten

- Read the *Touch and Feel: Puppy* or *Touch and Feel: Kitten* book with the child, letting him feel the pictures.
- Help the child open his hand and gently pet the stuffed animal. Say, "Gentle, gentle." Or, say, "Soft."

Touch Clothing

Materials
articles of clothing that correspond to the clothing represented in the *Touch and Feel: Clothes* book

- As you open each page, hold the real piece of clothing.
- Let the child explore how both textures feel.
- Describe and compare how they feel.

Something to Think About
As the children touch real objects and then compare them to the pictures in the book, they gradually learn that the pictures represent something that is real—that pictures are symbols, which is an important pre-reading skill.

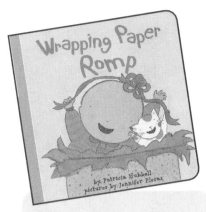

Wrapping Paper Romp

by Patricia Hubbell, illustrated by Jennifer Plecas

Story Synopsis

A bouncy rhyme depicts a baby having more fun with the wrapping paper and box than the present it contains. This story is an excellent example of a simple experience that is valuable and meaningful to a baby.

Reading Hints

Enjoy the rhythm and rhyme of the text as you read this to children. It's a good idea to practice reading this story aloud in front of a mirror before you read it to babies. Let the children discover what the kitty is doing on each page.

Story S-t-r-e-t-c-h-e-r: Music

Crumpled Paper

Materials
large sheets of paper

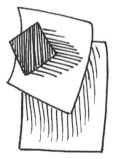

- Crumple paper into balls that will fit into children's hands.
- Let the children hold a paper ball in each hand.
- Let them hit the paper balls together and listen to the sound.
- Then let them do this while you play music.
- The paper balls make a nice soft sound that won't hurt the ears and still gives the children a feeling of making noise.

Story S-t-r-e-t-c-h-e-r: Object Play

Wrap It Up

Materials

toys from the classroom
used wrapping paper or colorful tissue paper
tape

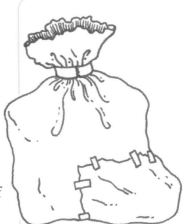

- While the children are asleep or out of the room, wrap some of their familiar toys with or without boxes.
- Let the children have the fun of unwrapping the toys and playing with the paper.

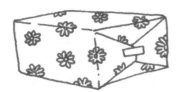 

Story S-t-r-e-t-c-h-e-r: Sensory

Tear Paper

Materials

old wrapping paper and paper grocery bags

- Help the children tear the paper.
- Listen to the sound of paper ripping.
- Stuff the torn paper into the paper grocery bag.
- Wash hands.

Note: Be sure children do not put small pieces of paper into their mouths.

Something to Think About

Unwrapping toys, crumpling paper, and tearing paper is a form of peekaboo. The child enjoys tearing and crumpling paper, hearing the noises it makes, and uncovering a surprise.

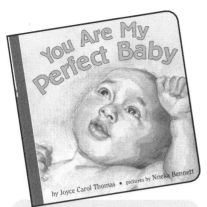

by Joyce Carol Thomas • pictures by Nneka Bennett

You Are My Perfect Baby

by Joyce Carol Thomas,
illustrated by Nneka Bennett

Story Synopsis

The text is a love poem. A mother marvels at her perfect baby and its perfect parts. A young baby will like to look at the pictures of the baby's face, and the reader will be reminded over and over that a baby is a true miracle!

Reading Hints

This book can be read anytime but especially when you are dressing or bathing the baby. Because it is a sturdy board book it will stand alone when opened, freeing your hands to dress the baby.

Story S-t-r-e-t-c-h-e-r: Music

Sing to the Baby

Materials

no special materials needed

■ As you engage in your daily routines, or when you are holding or rocking a baby, take the opportunity to sing to him. Any gentle tune or lullaby is fine.

■ It doesn't matter if you can carry a tune or not. The baby, held close, will enjoy the comforting vibrations of your voice.

Baby Foot Massage

Materials

baby lotion

- Gently rub baby lotion onto a child's feet and massage them while you sing to him.

Take Your Time

Materials

typical caregiving materials

- As you engage in the daily routines of feeding, diapering, washing infants' faces and hands, putting babies down for a nap, and so on try to slow down and move gently.
- This time is important for bonding and attachment.
- Talk to the babies, and let the babies respond.
- Enjoy the babies.

Something to Think About

While caring for a baby, it is important to slow down, step back, and occasionally marvel at this beautiful creation in your care. Singing to babies is helpful when transitioning from place to place or from one activity or routine to another. Soft music will help a tense, stressed baby to relax.

Chapter 3—Books for Toddlers

Using Books with Toddlers

Many teachers who begin reading to children as infants more or less give it up when the children become toddlers. Some of the complaints are that toddlers won't sit still for the whole book and that they keep grabbing the book away from the reader. They chew on books or throw them, or insist on turning a page back and forth.

It's true, toddlers are very busy, but toddlers can still enjoy books. Don't be too "formal" about reading at this age. Allow a child to take the book from you and examine it if she must. Don't insist on reading the book from beginning to end. Instead, follow the children's interest. You might just open the book randomly and name the objects on the page. Or talk about the book. "This book has an interesting shape, doesn't it? There are lots of pictures inside. There's even a picture of a doggie in this book."

One thing to remember is that toddlers are great mimics. They watch you very closely, and they want to be like you. So be sure to let them see you enjoying books yourself, reading for your own pleasure. And when you do read to the children, show your enthusiasm. Say something like, "I have a book here that's really fun. I like it a lot and I bet you will too. Let me show you what is inside of it."

Toddlers are also creatures of routine. They like things done in the same way every day. Routines give this large, uncertain world some predictability and help toddlers feel that they have a little bit of control over what happens in their world. Take advantage of this by establishing a regular routine for reading. They will learn to expect a book at certain times every day and are much more likely to settle down and enjoy it. Before naptime comes to mind first, of course, but there are many other times children could enjoy reading as part of the daily routine. Use books as a way to reconnect after being separated, as a way to settle down before lunchtime, or after coming in from active play outside.

Routines give this large, uncertain world some predictability and help toddlers feel that they have a little bit of control over what happens in their world.

The main thing to communicate is that books are fun.

As toddlers begin to say their first words, they enjoy pointing at familiar objects pictured in a book, or slapping the pictures and naming them. Keep in mind that children learn to understand words before they actually say them. Name an object pictured on the page in front of the child. "Where is the kitty on this page?" All the child has to do is understand the word "kitty" and point to it. Or, you could point to a picture and ask the child, "What's this?" Then the child can name the object for you. These two techniques develop different language skills—receptive language and expressive language.

Naming things pictured in a book also gives children some of their first experiences using symbols. A picture is a symbol for something that is real. Children recognize that the shape they see on the page represents some larger, three-dimensional object they have seen. This gives children a foundation for later using the symbols of letters and numbers.

Toddlers are also very interested in how books work. They love to turn the pages and open and close the book, making pictures appear and disappear. Books with lots of things to manipulate inside, such as flaps to lift, should be enjoyed with adult supervision because a toddler's heavy handling might destroy them. However, you can teach toddlers to turn pages carefully. When you start offering toddlers books with sturdy paper pages instead of board books, show them how to pick up the page from the edge between their thumb and forefinger and turn the page, rather than dragging their hand across the page. Show toddlers how to treat books with respect. Have a special shelf or box for them, and let them help you pick books up off the floor and place them carefully on the shelf.

The main thing to communicate is that books are fun. Toddlers are developing a sense of humor. They love to laugh. What tickles them is anything that is "incongruous," something a bit off, a bit "wacky." The examples we see over and over in children's books are animals acting like people, often wearing clothes and doing things people do. By this time, toddlers know that animals don't really wear clothes or walk on their hind legs, or talk, so it intrigues them and keeps their interest. Plus, illustrators often draw wonderful expressions on animals' faces. Toddlers also love silliness and making funny noises. They are learning that books can entertain and give people reasons to laugh.

Although a new book will always attract interest, you will find that toddlers like to hear the same book over and over again and will have certain favorites. They like the familiar. One of the best questions you can ask after reading a book is, "Shall we read it again?"

Techniques for Reading to Toddlers

- Make reading a pleasant, social experience.
- Cuddle up. Read to one child at a time or as a very small, cozy group.
- Don't force a child to stay with you to the end of the book, or even to read it from front to back.
- Point out familiar objects instead of reading the text if the story is too long or too complicated.
- Demonstrate that reading is a special experience by showing your own enthusiasm.
- Let the children choose the book whenever possible.
- Modify your language when you read. Slow down. Simplify the language or just point to things and name them, especially if you think the text is too advanced.
- Change your voice for different characters. Be expressive. Reflect the emotions in the text.
- Establish a reading routine, enjoying books at certain times each day.
- Have a special place for reading. Make it cozy and free of distractions.
- Even though you want to move the story along, let the children be actively involved and allow them to interrupt and ask questions.
- If a child brings you a book and asks you to read it, if you can, drop everything and read it.

Establish a reading routine, enjoying books at certain times each day.

Demonstrate that reading is a special experience by showing your own enthusiasm.

Books and S-t-r-e-t-c-h-e-r-s

All Fall Down
and
Tickle, Tickle
by Helen Oxenbury

Story Synopsis

These board books are larger than usual, about 8½ inches square. The illustrations are beautifully diverse, and drawn in a round and cuddly way that is very appealing. The sweet nature of babies and toddlers is revealed in their smiles and gestures. The double page spread is plenty of room to create the appearance of children that look big enough to jump off the pages. All Fall Down has children singing, running, and bouncing to a simple rhyming verse, and Tickle, Tickle depicts children playing in the mud, then taking a bath and dressing to a tickle time with lots of smiles at the end.

Reading Hints

These books are large and sturdy and will stand alone on a flat surface, such as a table or on the floor, if you want to hold two little ones while reading the story. Talk with the children about what is happening on each page. Older toddlers might reach for the book and smile in appropriate places. The illustrations have a "just like me" quality that toddlers will recognize.

Story S-t-r-e-t-c-h-e-r: Music and Movement

Singing

Material
favorite tape or CD of marching music
tape or CD player

- Gather the children around and put on the music.
- Listen to the music for a bit, and then begin to sing. Invite the children to sing with you.
- Get up and begin marching around in a circle on the rug.
- After all the children have joined the circle and are marching, add clapping to the routine. As the children get older, add different movements.
- Older children love to play the game of dropping to the floor just where you are when the music stops.

Float the Boats

Materials

large dishpan filled with water
small boats and toys that will float
towels

- Put the pan of water on the floor.
- Encourage one child or a small group of children to sit down on the floor around the pan of water.
- Give each child a boat or floating object and let them experiment with the pan of water and the boat. Remember that the concept of floating is new to them and they will be very excited to watch the boats float around. They may also want to splash the water and see what that feels like so have lots of towels handy. In warm weather it is fun to do this activity outside.

Note: Never leave the children alone with a pan or any size container of water.

Squishing in the Sand

Materials

large sandbox or beach
sand pails and shovels

- Let the toddlers crawl around in the sand so they can experience the feel of the sand on their bodies.
- Have a few sand toys, such as a small bucket and shovel for each child, so they can fill and empty their buckets while playing in the sand.

Note: This is a warm weather activity and one best done when the toddlers understand that sand is not good to eat.

Something to Think About

All children don't enjoy being tickled. It is best to begin with gentle tickles and to be sensitive to whether children enjoy them. If not, then stop! No more tickles.

Barnyard Dance!

by Sandra Boynton

Story Synopsis

All the animals in the barnyard get together for a dance. Each pair of animals has their turn on the dance floor to do their barnyard dance. They clap, stomp, twirl, bounce, swing, and prance. This is an active, lively story that is a toddler favorite!

Reading Hints

This book is more fun to read than you can imagine. It has spectacular rhyming words and phrases throughout. The action words in this book make you want to get up and move! Use your voice to enhance the wonderful rhymes the author has created. Toddlers will memorize the story after a very few readings, and will soon be able to say it with you.

Story S-t-r-e-t-c-h-e-r: Language

Name the Animal

Materials

no special materials needed

- Explain that you are going to read the story but you are going to leave some words out.
- Ask one child or a small group of children to say the word if they know it.
- In the story the action word is always first and the animal name is second. They will learn very quickly that the horse bows, the pig twirls, and so on.
- It will be fun for one child or several to shout out the name of the animal that does the particular action you are reading. This s-t-r-e-t-c-h-e-r- is loud but fun!

Movement Game

Materials

no special materials needed

- Suggest to the toddlers who are listening to the story that as you read the story they can pretend to do the action that you are reading about.
- They can clap, stomp, bow, twirl, bounce, spin, and so on.
- You may need to do the motions the first few times until they understand the actions that go with each word.
- Read it more slowly when you first start doing the movements until they get the idea of the game.

Toddlers can slap, stomp, bow, twirl, bounce, and spin.

Old MacDonald Had a Farm

Materials

no special materials needed

- If you play an instrument, play it with this song, or just sing the words to "Old MacDonald Had a Farm" very slowly a couple of times.
- Invite the children to join in the next time and repeat the phrases and then sing them until they have learned the words.
- Learning this song can take place over a period of days, adding a verse each day or whenever you think the children are ready for another verse.

Something to Think About

Barnyard Dance! provides a look at farm animals, and lots of movement and action, all of which toddlers really enjoy. Assess the children's interest and determine whether you should do more animal experiences over the coming days or even weeks. Building language and learning experiences on the children's interests will accomplish more growth for the children than imposing an experience that is not something they are really interested in at that particular time.

The Bear Went Over the Mountain

by Rosemary Wells

Story Synopsis

This is the simple story of the bear wanting to know what was on the other side of the mountain. Rosemary Wells has added her own special touch by illustrating the specific action of the bear opposite each page with a phrase of the song and added a different flower on each spread.

Reading Hints

Ask the children to notice that the bear is carrying a basket. When he starts over the mountain the basket is empty. Some children will notice that the basket is full of flowers when he greets his mother.

Story S-t-r-e-t-c-h-e-r: Music

Sing "The Bear Went Over the Mountain"

Materials

no special materials needed

■ Sing "The Bear Went Over the Mountain" to add to the pretending experience.
■ It is an easy song to make very funny by holding some words longer than others and some faster. It makes for a very funny time, which toddlers love.

Being a Bear

Materials
no special materials needed

- After reading the story, invite the toddlers to join you as you pretend to be bears climbing over the mountain.
- Do the motions of climbing with both hands and feet in the position of a climber, and hold your hands above your eyes, as if to see far off, when you get to the top and can see the other side.
- Add your own creative motions to different parts of the story.
- Encourage the children to repeat the rhyme with you and they will associate the meaning of the words with the motions.

Pretend to be bears climbing over the mountain.

Story S-t-r-e-t-c-h-e-r: Sensory

Gift of Flowers

Materials
flowers
basket

- Talk to one child or a small group of children about the flowers that appear on every page of the story.
- Ask them about the bear's basket. Why was it empty when he started up the mountain? Why was it full when he came down? What did he do with the basket of flowers?
- Talk about how flowers are special, and when we want to do something very nice for another person we might give them flowers.
- If there is a place to pick flowers it would be a nice thing for the toddlers to pick some flowers, put them in a basket, and choose someone to give the flowers.

Something to Think About

Helping young children develop empathy is a worthwhile thing to do. Understanding that when someone feels bad that we can help him or her to feel better is an important concept that children can begin to understand with a story such as this. Honoring another person or celebrating children's achievement is another occasion for a small gift of flowers.

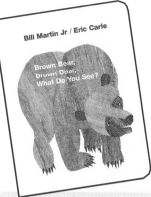

Brown Bear, Brown Bear, What Do You See?

by Bill Martin, Jr., illustrated by Eric Carle

Story Synopsis

This board book is about a variety of animals that ask, "What do you see?" Brown Bear, who is featured on the cover, answers the question at the end of the book. The other animals are a red bird, yellow duck, blue horse, green frog, purple cat, white dog, black sheep, and goldfish. Eric Carle's bold illustrations cover a two-page spread. The cover shows Brown Bear facing the reader and the back cover shows Brown Bear from the back.

Reading Hints

Show the child the cover of the book. Notice that Brown Bear is facing toward us on the front and going away from us on the back. Let the child turn the pages of the board book and wait to see if the child labels the animals. When the child says, "bird," add "red bird." When the child says, "duck," add "yellow duck." Laugh about the funny colors of the blue horse and the purple cat. After perusing the book from cover to cover, read the book.

Story S-t-r-e-t-c-h-e-r: Language

Colors and Names

Materials
book
colored construction paper
scissors

■ Look through the book with one child or a small group of children. Let them tell you the names of the animals. If they say, "horsey," or "birdey," accept these names, but also encourage them to say the color names. You may hear them begin to use the shorter name, horse, when they say "blue horse," rather than "horsey."

■ Cut strips of construction paper to match the colors of the animals—brown, red, blue, green, purple, white, black, and gold.

■ Let a child select a color from the array of strips. Go to the page and read about the color that the child selects. For example, if the child selects the black strip, then turn to the black sheep and read that page.

Clap for Brown Bear

Materials
book

- Read the book again and set up the easy rhythm of the question and answers.
- Clap and pause, alternating between clapping the question while looking at the picture and saying the answer together.

Story S-t-r-e-t-c-h-e-r: Sensory

Fingerpainting Brown Bear and Friends

Freezer paper shiny side up!

Materials
old clothes
tape
fingerpaint paper or freezer paper
fingerpaints
clothesline
clothespins

- Tape the fingerpaint paper or freezer paper onto a tabletop with the shiny side up.
- Provide fingerpaints of the colors found in *Brown Bear, Brown Bear, What Do You See?*
- Let one child or a small group of children select one of the colors of the animals and simply let them enjoy the fingerpainting. While they are painting, mention, "Emily, I see you are painting with yellow, like, 'Yellow Duck, Yellow Duck, What Do You See?'"
- After a child has finished her fingerpainting, hang it up on a clothesline to dry.

Something to Think About

Let the toddlers take turns selecting a construction paper strip and hearing their color pages read from *Brown Bear, Brown Bear, What Do You See?* During the "Clap for Brown Bear" Story S-t-r-e-t-c-h-e-r, let one toddler stand up and hold her color strip while the other children clap the rhythm to that section of the book.

Bus, Plane, Train, and Ship
by Chris L. Demarest

Story Synopsis

*Each of these four little square board books is devoted to a different mode of transportation. The concepts have been carefully developed using action words and phrases that toddlers will enjoy. Each story involves a trip complete with all the sites from beginning to end. For example, **Train** begins with "engine up front" and ends with "home at last!" The bold colorful illustrations enhance these travel action stories.*

Reading Hints

Exciting adventures can be conjured up by telling your own story using the words and phrases on each page. Use your best voice to make the sounds included in the telling of each story. Toddlers will also want to help with these sounds.

Story S-t-r-e-t-c-h-e-r: Language

Go for a Bus Ride

Materials

city bus

- The *Bus* story is about a bus ride in the city.
- A ride on a city bus would be a great s-t-r-e-t-c-h-e-r.
- The riders will see many of the same things in the story on a ride through any town in the United States.
- Use the language from the book as you journey on the bus.
- Talk about your adventure as you are traveling.

Be an Airplane

Materials

no special materials needed

- This stretcher is more fun out of doors or in a large open space.
- Show toddlers how to stretch their arms out as wide as possible and then run fast like an airplane, holding their arms straight and stiff.
- Pretending to be an airplane is lots of fun for toddlers. Be sure to check the area and be sure that it is safe for running.
- A large green grassy space or sandy beaches are wonderful places to play airplane.

Pretending to be an airplane is lots of fun for toddlers.

Make a Train

Materials

shoeboxes
hole punch
heavy string
markers or crayons

- After reading *Train,* it will be fun to make a shoebox train.
- Draw windows and wheels and any other parts on the boxes to make the train cars.
- Punch a hole in the ends of each box, and thread the string through all the boxes.
- Tie a knot at the beginning and at the end of the train. Be sure to leave a piece of string long enough for toddlers to pull the train.
- A visit to a real train station, or a real train ride would of course be the ultimate s-t-r-e-t-c-h-e-r for this book.
- The vocabulary from the book could easily be reinforced on such a journey.

Something to Think About

Toddlers need movement, and it is sometimes difficult to provide them with all the activity they need. This series of books has unlimited possibilities for songs, rhymes, and other activities that will enhance the movement adventures you create with them. A great resource for movement ideas is *Wiggle, Giggle, and Shake* by Rae Pica.

Clap Hands
and
Say Goodnight
by Helen Oxenbury

Story Synopsis

Clap Hands and Say Goodnight are two titles in the Helen Oxenbury jumbo board book series. These titles feature beautifully illustrated round, cuddly babies and toddlers. Each group of infants and toddlers are involved in typical activities. However, even though they are together, they are each involved in individual activities, as is so typical of this age. With an occasional acknowledgment of the friends, you will see them clapping, dancing and spinning around, eating, making music, waving, crawling up and down on dad, swinging, riding daddy's back around the room, and falling asleep.

Reading Hints

This series is ready for the kind of use that toddlers give to books, from carrying around for hours and hours to dropping them here and there. Place these books on the bookshelf where children can choose to look at them on their own. These books are excellent choices for young children who are beginning to tell stories. These children have a lot to say and the illustrations in these books will help them express it.

Story S-t-r-e-t-c-h-e-r: Movement

Swinging in the Park

Materials

park or playground with safety swings for young children
adequate number of adults to help with the children

■ This is an activity to do with toddlers who are walking independently.
■ Bundle up in coats and hats if the weather is cold, and walk to a park or playground that has those wonderful swings for infants and toddlers, the kind that are protected on all four sides. Some even have seat belts.
■ Give each child a ride on the swing.

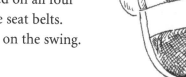

Story S-t-r-e-t-c-h-e-r: Music

Sitting Band

Materials

wooden spoons
small saucepans
toilet paper rolls

- Sit with the children on the rug and tell them that you are going to give them an instrument to use while you make music together with the materials. When you first introduce these instruments, it is a good idea for the children to sit down while playing the instruments.
- When you are confident the children are ready for the next step, introduce the concept of a "marching band."
- Show them the picture in the book of the children playing music.
- Give each child either a toilet paper roll to use for a trumpet or horn, or a saucepan and wooden spoon to use for a drum
- Make sure you also have an instrument and march with them while they make music.
- Talk with them about what they are doing to develop their vocabulary regarding music and musical instruments.

Give each child either a toilet paper roll to use for a trumpet or horn, or a saucepan and wooden spoon to use for a drum.

Story S-t-r-e-t-c-h-e-r: Music and Movement

Dance and Spin

Materials
Record, tape or CD player
Record, tape or CD

- Play "dancing" music.
- Spinning is the main word for this activity. Since you probably have danced with the children before, they will know what to do when you say, "We're going to dance now."
- Introduce the children to the fun of spinning by picking up each child and, while you hold them, doing a little spin around the room.
- Give each child a turn to spin with you or other adults who are participating in the activity.
- For children who are able, let them spin by themselves. They will probably try to help each other spin.

Note: Be sure you have an open area away from tables, chairs, or hard surfaces in case the children fall down, which they most probably will. A special area rug with big pillows marking off the perimeter is a perfect place for dancing and spinning.

Something to Think About
Young children who have just started walking want to be on the move constantly and do not always give the impression that they are tired. It is only after you provide them with a quiet restful activity that they, and often times you, realize they need to rest. It is very important to balance a toddler's day with both active and restful experiences.

Clap Your Hands

by Lorinda Bryan Cauley

Story Synopsis

A host of costumed animals combined with a merry bunch of children make this a delightful book. The rhyming story is perfect for an action-packed story time any time the book is read. The illustrations are so realistic and lively they almost jump off the page.

Reading Hints

This is a story to be read just before an active play time, or on a rainy day when active outdoor play is limited or not possible. It is not a story for the quieter times of day, such as before naptime or meals.

Story S-t-r-e-t-c-h-e-r: Language

Secret Surprise

Materials

a surprise such as a small toddler-safe toy or a silly picture of a costumed animal

■ Whisper in one child's ear.
■ See if the child can whisper also.
■ Whisper in her ear, "I have a surprise!"
■ See if the child can follow a simple direction you whisper. ("Look behind the bookshelf. There's a surprise waiting there.")

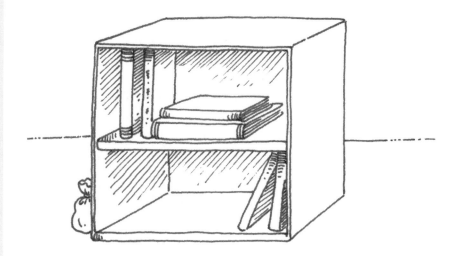

Follow the Leader

Materials
no special materials needed

- Play this game with several children. Toddlers love imitating older children or adults.
- Let one child think of some fun movement or sound.
- If necessary, suggest a movement to the toddler that everyone can imitate.
- At first you might just all do something the child does spontaneously.
- She will love the feeling of power when everyone does what she is doing.

Toddlers love imitating older children or adults.

Dance the Story to Music

Materials
lively instrumental recorded music

- After the children are familiar with the book and have demonstrated the various movements on the pages, suggest you "dance" the book.
- Play recorded music and read the book, letting the child act out the motions to the music.
- The more children participating in this, the more fun.

Something to Think About

Toddlers love demonstrating their new physical skills. And they also love being active and being silly. This is a rather long action story so you may need to read only a few pages at one sitting. Take your cues from the group who is listening to the story. Be alert to their interest in the story.

Diggers and Dumpers and Fire Engine

by Snapshot

Story Synopsis

These books are full color photographs of all kinds of trucks and fire engines. Most are common trucks and fire engines, but there are some unusual ones such as the airport fire engine that carries its own water. These sturdy board books are shaped like a dump truck and a fire engine. This feature allows them to be used as a toy truck or toy fire engine.

Reading Hints

These books of photographs lend themselves to lively discussions with toddlers about the trucks and fire engines pictured. Good questions can help toddlers develop the concept of what these machines look like and their enormous size and power. Comparisons to familiar things, such as the children's houses or cars, will enhance their concept of big and even bigger.

Story S-t-r-e-t-c-h-e-r: Language

Fire House Visit

Materials
no special materials needed

■ Call your local firehouse and ask if you can come and visit.
■ Ask how many adults and children can come at one time.
■ Ask them to talk with the toddlers about fire safety while you are there.
■ Take the *Fire Engine* book along to see if they have any trucks like the ones in the book.
■ This is a good lesson on comparisons and differences, which are important concepts to be learned.

Playing with Trucks

Materials

toy trucks

- After reading the story, gather the toy trucks and put them on a nice hard surface such as a wooden floor or a cement walk.
- Let the children play with the trucks.
- You might help the children build a ramp with a flat board so the trucks will have an incline plane to roll down.
- If there is a construction site close by, walking to the site to see the big diggers and dumpers in action would be a special treat.

Learning about Yellow

Materials

fingerpaint paper
paint shirts
yellow fingerpaints

- Set up a table with yellow fingerpaint and fingerpaint paper.
- Read *Diggers and Dumpers*, talking about the colors of the heavy equipment.
- The children may realize that a lot of the trucks are yellow and may even ask why.
- Talk with them about other things that are yellow.
- When you have finished your discussion, put paint shirts on the toddlers to protect their clothes from the fingerpaint.
- Go to the table with fingerpaint and paper.
- Give them plenty of time to explore the yellow paint and to make all the yellow things they want to make before cleaning up and laying their papers out to dry.

Something to Think About

Trucks and fire engines are big to toddlers. If they are unfamiliar with these vehicles, they may have questions for several days about the books and the s-t-r-e-t-c-h-e-r-s you do with them. Some young children are fascinated with dump trucks, and they make this their primary play focus for a long time. Be prepared to talk with them and help them develop the concepts on which they are working.

Families
by Debbie Bailey, photographs by Susan Huszar

Story Synopsis

Brilliant color photographs of children and their mothers, fathers, brothers, sisters, grandpas, and grandmas, doing all the things families do together. The book is divided into six different sections, one for each member of the family.

Reading Hints

Reading the entire book would be too much for any toddler. Reading a section at a time and giving full attention to that person would be a good way to read this book. It could be read on six different days. The photographs are active so it will be interesting to tell a story about the pictures, or elicit stories from the children about what is happening in the photos.

Story S-t-r-e-t-c-h-e-r: Language

Sharing about Families

Materials
photographs of families
poster board
glue

- Ask parents to bring in family photographs and each day, give one toddler a chance to share pictures of her family. If possible and appropriate, ask the child questions about her family.
- Be sensitive to the different configurations of families and help the children to celebrate the diversity of their families.
- Make a poster of all the photographs and hang it on the wall where the children can see it.

Grandparent Volunteers

Materials
grandparents

- Find a grandmother and/or a grandfather who can come and spend a day or even part of a day in the classroom.
- Ask them to do the things that you do each day—reading, talking, playing, singing, and so on.
- This will let the toddlers know that grandparents are caring, wonderful people who are interested in them and what they do every day.

Party for Families

Materials
food and decorations

- Plan a simple party and invite families to come by one afternoon about an hour before it is time to go home.
- Discuss the idea with the children, of having a party to "Celebrate Families," and let them help with the planning and getting ready for the party.

Something to Think About

Families come in all sizes, shapes, and colors. Celebrating diverse families and helping families to appreciate each other is a wonderful goal for any school or program.

Have You Seen My Duckling?

by Nancy Tafuri

Story Synopsis

There are only two phrases in this Caldecott Honor book, yet the story is complete. It begins with one adventurous baby duckling swimming away from the nest while the other seven watch. The seven left behind seem to be telling mother duck what happened. The remainder of the story is about the mother duck and her brood of seven visiting the various inhabitants of the pond to ask, "Have you seen my duckling?" In each scene, the lost duck is barely visible, but is somewhere in the picture. Tafuri's texturing of the feathers, expressions, and renderings of pond life create a terrific counting adventure.

Reading Hints

Show the children the cover of the book and count the number of baby ducks. This almost wordless picture book can be told while the children attempt to see the little adventurous duckling who is barely seen. For young children who are at the pointing stage, let them point to the little duck. Tell the story, perhaps making up some dialogue between the mother duck and the crane, turtle, beaver, and catfish.

Story S-t-r-e-t-c-h-e-r: Movement and Music

Quack, Quack, Quack

Materials

no special materials needed

■ Teach the children the words to "Five Little Ducks."

> Five little ducks that I once knew,
> Big ones, little ones, skinny ones, too,
>
> Refrain:
> But the one little duck with the feather on his back,
> All he could do was 'Quack, Quack, Quack.'
> All he could do was 'Quack, Quack, Quack.'
>
> Down to the river they would go,
> Waddling, waddling, to and fro.
>
> (Refrain)
>
> Up from the river they would come,
> Ho, ho, ho, ho, hum, hum, hum
>
> (Refrain)

■ If desired, adapt the hand motions as described in *Marc Brown's Favorite Hand Rhymes* (see page 186).

Water Table Pond

Materials

water table
small buckets or pails
rocks
clumps of grasses with soil attached (optional)
blue and green tempera paint or food coloring
any plastic models of pond animals (optional)
rubber ducks

- Fill the water table with clean water.
- Let the children add blue and green tempera paint to give the water the pond color.
- If desired, place clumps of grass in the pails and place around the edges of the water table. If necessary, add rocks in the bottom of the pails to keep them down in the water.
- Let the children play with their floating ducks and other plastic animals in the pond.

Pond Pictures

Materials

bluish-green watercolor paint
paintbrushes
watercolor paper or manila paper
masking tape
newspapers
margarine tubs
water

- Tape the newspapers to the tabletop.
- Tape the watercolor or manila paper onto the newspapers that cover the tabletop.
- Demonstrate how to wet the watercolor brush and dip it into the watercolor.
- Encourage the children to paint pond water.

Something to Think About

When toddlers and twos are first starting to use art materials, they are in the exploration stage. They simply enjoy the medium and experiment with it. Many, simply will enjoy the process of covering the entire sheet of paper with the water or brushing the paint on the paper.

Here Are My Hands

by Bill Martin, Jr. and John Archambault, illustrated by Ted Rand

Story Synopsis

A simple verse that captures the feelings of young children as they notice all the different parts of their bodies, from "hands for catching and throwing" to the "skin that bundles me." The rhymes and Rand's illustrations combine to make a lovely book. Children from different ethnic backgrounds are warmly and sensitively depicted through chalk drawings.

Reading Hints

Before showing the children the cover of the book, point to different body parts and have the children identify that body part. Older ones can say what they do with that body part. Show the cover of the book and notice the six children and what they are doing, catching a ball with a mitt, ballerina dancing, and so on.

Story S-t-r-e-t-c-h-e-r: Movement and Music

Motions to the Rhyme

Materials

no special materials needed

- Use motions of the story and turn the rhyme into a chant.
- Let the children demonstrate the actions with their body parts. For example, in the book the phrase is "Here are my hands for catching and throwing," encourage the children to hold up their hands and pretend to catch or throw a ball.
- Sit and hold your feet in your hands while saying, "Here are my feet, for stopping and going."
- Point to your head and say, "Here is my head, for thinking and knowing."
- After the children have rehearsed the motions to the rhyme in the book, read the book again without demonstrating the motions. Let them take their cues from the words and pictures in the book.

Story S-t-r-e-t-c-h-e-r: Object Play

Button, Zip, and Snap

Materials

clothes that button, zip, and snap
pieces of plywood
stapler
duct tape

- Children like to dress themselves, but they sometimes have difficulty doing more than pulling on pants.
- To help them develop dexterity, dress some dolls or a teddy bear with clothes that have large buttons, zippers, or snaps.
- Construct dressing frames by stapling fabric that has zippers, buttons or snaps onto pieces of plywood or wooden picture frames. Cover all rough edges and staples with duct tape.

Hand Prints

Materials
plaster of Paris mix (available from craft stores)
measuring cup
water
large mixing bowl
one meat tray per child
pencil
paper towels
table
newspaper

- Cover the top of a table with newspaper for easy cleanup.
- Mix the plaster of Paris as directed on the package, usually one part water to two parts plaster.
- Pour the plaster into three or four meat trays at a time.
- Use one meat tray for each child.
- When the plaster begins to harden, usually in about ten minutes, make the handprint.
- Hold one child's hand loosely and guide the child in making the handprint.
- Before the plaster hardens, carve the child's name and the date in the plaster with a pencil point that has no lead in it. Also poke a hole in the top of the plaster to hang when dry.

Something to Think About

Here Are My Hands is an excellent book to extend the body awareness process. Toddlers are enjoying their newfound abilities and increasing coordination. Place a full-length unbreakable mirror horizontally so the children can see themselves easily as they practice movements to *Here Are My Hands*.

Hey! Wake Up!

by Sandra Boynton

Story Synopsis

The animals are asleep; they awaken to a rollicking rhyme of actions they need to do as they go through their morning routines of dressing, eating, and playing.

Reading Hints

All of Sandra Boynton's books are fun to read; they are both visual and auditory treats for toddlers. As with all of her books, she writes words with feelings that need to be expressed and draws pictures that are humorous and delightful to see. Hold the book so that the children have a good view of every page as you read.

Story S-t-r-e-t-c-h-e-r: Language

Morning Wake Up

Materials
no special materials needed

■ After you have read the story several times, suggest to one child or a small group of children that they might want to listen to the words you are reading, and see if they can do the actions as you read them.
■ These actions include opening their eyes, yawning, stretching, and wiggling, all fun things that toddlers like to do.
■ This is a good book to read at the beginning of the day.

Story S-t-r-e-t-c-h-e-r: Movement

Play Outside

Materials
ball

■ Talk with the children about how the animals played outside after they had breakfast.
■ Then go outside and play.

- The animals in the book played ball, so you might take a ball and roll the ball back and forth between you and the children.
- Swings and other equipment on the playground may interest the children, and if so, save the ball for another time.

Make Breakfast

Materials
orange juice
cereal
milk
bread
butter
jelly
glasses
bowls
plates
spoons
knives
napkins

- Making meals together encourages toddlers to eat, because they like to eat what they have prepared.
- The animals' breakfast in the book is orange juice, cereal, and toast, and the rabbit has broccoli stew.
- Make an early morning snack (breakfast) with the children.
- You might want to discuss how different people or animals eat different things, and describe the way things smell, taste, and feel while you are eating this breakfast.
- Unless you have a rabbit joining you for breakfast you won't have to make broccoli stew!

Something to Think About

Having a routine is a positive thing for toddlers. Knowing what is going to happen next gives toddlers the sense that the world is an orderly place.

I Went Walking

by Sue Williams, illustrated by Julie Vivas

Story Synopsis

In the delightful, humorous, and bright illustrations of this board book, a child goes walking and gathers an entourage of animals who follow along. A repeated pattern book, the child can predict what will happen next.

Reading Hints

Each page has a clue in the illustrations about what is going to happen on the next page. Ask the children, "What will the child see next?"

Story S-t-r-e-t-c-h-e-r: Language

Magnet Board Story

Materials
self-stick magnetic strips
poster board
scissors
markers
cookie sheet or other metal surface

■ Draw an outline of the animals in the book, color with markers, cut them out, and attach magnetic strips to the backs of the outlines.

■ As you read the story, let one child at a time pick out the animal mentioned on the page and stick it on the magnet board.

Animal Parade

Materials

no special materials needed

- Encourage a small group of children, one at a time, to pretend to be the animals in the book. "Let's pretend you're a cat. How would you move? How does a cat sound? Now pretend to be a cow..."
- As you read the story, name a child to be each new animal.
- The child pretends to be the animal and then lines up behind the child who was the previous animal. (If you have more children than animals in the group, name two children for some of the animals.)
- When you have finished the story, the line-up of "animals" can parade around.

Real Animals

Materials

no special materials needed

- Visit a farm or petting zoo in your community to see live examples of the animals illustrated in the book.
- If possible, help the children pet the animals, and comment on how the animals look, feel, and smell.

Something to Think About

This book is a representation of real life mathematics. One animal at a time is added, and the line following the child gets longer and longer.

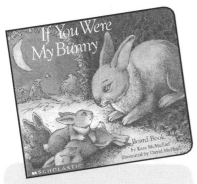

If You Were My Bunny

by Kate McMullan, illustrated by David McPhail

Story Synopsis

If You Were My Bunny is the story of how mama bunny, mama bear, mama cat, mama duck, and mama dog would comfort their babies. After each scene between mama and baby, there is a song to be read or sung in lullaby form. McPhail's illustrations of pen and ink with watercolor washes set just the right soft and warm tone denoting emotional security.

Reading Hints

Find a cozy spot with soft pillows or a favorite chair. Invite one child over and after she crawls up into your lap, place *If You Were My Bunny* into the child's hands. Let the child hold the board book and turn the pages, noting the different animals. Start to hum one of the lullabies, and then say that you are going to read and sing this book. If the toddler becomes distracted, stop reading and let her get down and explore something else and come back to you. If you sense the child is becoming distracted, only read the first part of the book, then simply look at the pages of the rest of the book, noting the names of the animals.

Story S-t-r-e-t-c-h-e-r: Language

The Names of the Animals

Materials
book

- After the children are familiar with the book, ask them to point to the mama animals and the baby animals as you read the book. If the children are having difficulty pointing, guide their fingers.
- After reading the book through, go back to the illustrations and let the children point out each mama and baby. Emphasize the baby animal's names, such as "little cottontail," "bear cub," "kitten," "duckling," and "puppy."

Bunny's Lullaby

Materials
book

- Read the bunny section of *If You Were My Bunny.*
- Sing the bunny's lullaby.
- Select one child's favorite animal from the book and learn that lullaby. Sing it together.
- Rock the child in rhythm to the lullaby.
- At another time, sing the lullaby as a "call" for the child to come and read the book with you.

Story S-t-r-e-t-c-h-e-r: Pretending

Falling Asleep

Materials
pillows
favorite blanket
teddy bear

- At the end of *If You Were My Bunny*, the mother puts the child to bed and the child falls asleep with a teddy bear.
- After each animal scene, pretend to fall asleep and encourage the children to pretend with you. For example, yawn and stretch, then cuddle up and close your eyes.
- At the end of the book after the child's scene, let the children find their favorite blanket or quilt and stuffed animal, then let them pretend to be falling asleep.
- If the children go to sleep with the pretending, let them sleep.

Something to Think About

Watch to see if the children notice the details in the illustrations and label them. McPhail's illustrations highlight some of the words. For example, there is a spotlight on the "buzzing bee" in the lullaby when Mama Bunny sings, "If that clover's buzzing with a bee, Mama's going to bring you some dandelion tea." If the children do not notice, point out the details in some of the pictures, and then they will begin to do the same.

Jesse Bear, What Will You Wear?

*by Nancy White Carlstrom,
illustrated by Bruce Degan*

Story Synopsis

Carlstrom's cheerful rhyming story follows Jesse Bear from the beginning of the day when he is gettting dressed for play, until the night when he is tucked in right with his teddy bear. Throughout the day, Mother Bear asks, "Jesse Bear, what will you wear?" He answers in rhyme and sometimes it is not clothes he is wearing but sand in his pants, rice in his hair, and bubbles on his tummy in the tub. Degen's illustrations convey loving, accepting feelings in this humanized bear family and their home. The colors are warm and bright, and each scene is rich with details of home life and outside play.

Reading Hints

Read the title, "Jesse Bear, What Will You Wear?" Ask the children to tell you what they are wearing. Ask one child if what she is wearing is her favorite shirt. Read the story and pause for the toddlers to comment on the different pictures and point out details. The rhyming helps to push the story along so the children may prefer to hear the whole story, then go back to explore the details in the picture. Pause in the middle of the book to discuss the bear swinging and father coming home.

Story S-t-r-e-t-c-h-e-r: Language

Flannel Board Story of *Jesse Bear, What Will You Wear?*

Materials

flannel board

felt pieces of Jesse, underwear with stars on it, blue pants, red shirt, a bib, light blue pajamas, tiny teddy bear, Mother Bear, Father Bear

■ Read *Jesse Bear, What Will You Wear?*

■ On another day, tell the story using the flannel board pieces.

■ Make the felt pieces, the flannel board, and the book available to the children.

■ Encourage the children to begin retelling the story in their own words using the flannel board pieces.

■ Some will simply play with the flannel board pieces, which is fine.

Jesse's Sandbox

Materials

sand table or sandbox
dump truck, sand buckets, and shovels

- Show the children the picture of Jesse Bear in the sandbox outside.
- Let the children collect their favorite sandbox objects.
- Leave them to their own play.
- When it is clean-up time, talk about how Jesse had to shake the sand out of the clothes and brush himself off. As they shake and brush, call them Jesse Bears.

Pretend to Be Jesse Bear

Materials

large size blue shorts or pants
red shirt
bib
pajamas
unbreakable mirror

- Place the clothes in an area near a mirror.
- Let the children pretend to be Jesse Bear getting dressed by putting the clothes over their own.
- While the children are dressing ask, "Jesse Bear, what will you wear?"
- Talk about what the children wear in the morning, at noon, or at night.

Something to Think About

Young children begin making choices as toddlers when they decide what they want to wear. It is important to give children many opportunities to make choices, such as which book to read, game to play, snack to eat, and so on.

More!, and Uh Oh!

by Sheilagh Noble,

and

Whoops!

by Louise Batchelor

Story Synopsis

These books have a typical toddler theme that will be immediately recognizable. The stories are filled with many of the words and first phrases that most toddlers have learned. It is easy to tell the story from the pictures using the simple words given for the stories' actions. Uh Oh! is a story about a little girl's first day at nursery school. In Whoops! two toddlers celebrate a birthday with their mothers while learning to share and use the words they know and enjoy. A walk in the park, enjoying other toddlers, swinging, and talking with animals makes More! a delightful story.

Reading Hints

It is fun to personalize these stories. Give the children and parents in the stories names of people that are known to the toddlers. Tell the story while using the word or phrase found on each page. After a few tellings, children will begin to name the people in the stories and look forward to the antics each book expresses.

Story S-t-r-e-t-c-h-e-r: Language and Sensory

Chocolate Pudding (Uh Oh!)

Materials

chocolate pudding ingredients
bowls
spoons

- Make a simple chocolate pudding with the children.
- As you eat the pudding, the words "yum," "messy," and "squishy" are sure to be used, just as they are in the book.

A Walk in the Park (More!)

Materials

no special materials needed

- Take a walk to a neighborhood park and visit with other children and animals in the park.
- A park with swings would make the visit like the park in the story.

Birthday Party (Whoops!)

Materials

paper streamers
party hats
pretend presents
dolls

- Help the children stage a birthday party, and act it out with their dolls.
- Use the words from the book during your conversation at the pretend party.

Something to Think About

For a child who seems to enjoy the words and has begun to recognize them you can make vocabulary cards on index cards. Print one word on each card, punch a hole in the corner of the cards and put them on a shower curtain ring. Children enjoy carrying their ring around, reading the words on the cards, and watching the ring fill with their words.

My First Songs

*collected and illustrated
by Jane Manning*

Story Synopsis

*My First Songs includes
favorite songs that are fun for
toddlers to sing. "Ring around
the Rosie," "London Bridge,"
"Pop! Goes the Weasel," "Hush
Little Baby," "Old MacDonald
Had a Farm," "The Eentsy,
Weentsy Spider," and
"Twinkle, Twinkle Little Star"
are all included. An
illustration of each song is
included on the left-hand page
with the words for the song on
the right. The illustrations are
full page and in excellent color
and provide a clear "picture"
of the songs and their
meaning.*

Reading Hints

Most adults will recognize the songs and will literally sing their way through this book. Children should be encouraged to clap their hands, tap their feet, and make other rhythmic motions as you sing the songs. Young toddlers will respond best if you limit the number of songs per reading to only two or three different songs until they have learned each one. This is a book that will be used almost daily until the toddlers have added all the songs to their repertoire. They will enjoy clapping and tapping each time they see this book and should be encouraged to move freely as they sing.

Story St-r-e-t-c-h-e-r: Music

Star Gazing

Materials
plastic glow-in-the-dark stars

- A fun thing to do with stars is to put plastic glow-in-the-dark stars on the ceiling of a room.
- This can be done in the daytime by putting them on the ceiling of a large closet or using shades in a room to block out the light.
- These stars come in little packages of assorted sizes.
- Surprise the children by putting the stars on the ceiling after they have gone home on the day you read the book.
- On the next day read the book just before naptime.
- Turn out the light and see if the children notice the stars before you mention them.

Story St-r-e-t-c-h-e-r: Music

"The Wheels on the Bus"

Materials
local bus

- Teach the children the words to "The Wheels on the Bus," which is included in the book.
- Also teach them the sounds and motions for each of the verses. This should be done over several days as there are six verses.
- When the song is familiar, this is a good opportunity for a bus ride.
- There are many concepts to be learned in this song and taking a ride on a local or neighborhood bus would give the child an opportunity to explore the "town," things that are "round" and develop an understanding of buses and their importance in our communities.
- Young children love this song.

Story S-t-r-e-t-c-h-e-r: Pretending

Make a Pretend Rowboat

Materials

two cardboard wrapping paper rolls and one pillow for each child
string or masking tape and scissors, optional

- Line pillows up on the floor to make a rowboat.
- If necessary, make an outline of a rowboat using string or strips of masking tape.
- Lay the pillows on the floor in a line.
- "Talk the children" into the boat, being careful as they step inside the boat and sit down easily, so the boat won't rock.
- Give each child a set of wrapping paper rolls to use for oars.
- Add other descriptive dialogue to make the rowboat trip as much of an adventure as you like, such as being sure to wear hats to keep the sun off your faces, and so on.
- When you are all in the boat you are ready to sing and row until you reach your destination.

Something to Think About

Providing stories and songs with repetitive phrases is important for young children. Repetition stimulates both receptive language skills (listening) and expressive language skills (speaking), which are critical in children's literacy development.

On Mother's Lap

by Ann Herbert Scott,
illustrated by Glo Coalson

Story Synopsis

A Native Alaskan mother always has room on her lap. Her little boy keeps adding favorite toys and even a puppy to the cozy setting, snuggling in each time. However, when his little brother wants to join him on Mother's lap, he announces that there's not enough room.

Reading Hints

It would be great to read this book while rocking a child on your lap. The child could join you chanting the repeated phrase about rocking back and forth.

Story S-t-r-e-t-c-h-e-r: Object Play

What Fits?

Materials

different toys and other objects

- Let one child (or a small group of children) see how many things she (or they) can put on your lap while you are sitting down before things start falling off.

What Fits Where?

Materials

container such as a cardboard box or a laundry basket
toys and objects

- Toddlers are still figuring out the relationships of size and space. Playing with containers is a fascinating and a wonderful way to explore size and space relationships.
- Suggest that the children try to put the toys (or other objects) in the container.
- Ask, "Do you think it will all fit?"
- Let the children guess, and then help them put the toys and objects in the container to test to see if their guesses were right.

What Can Fit on My Lap?

Materials

child-sized rocking chair
various toys and objects (try to match the toys in the book)

- Let the child pretend to be the mother in the story and sit in a child-sized rocking chair.
- As you read the book, tuck each object in turn onto the child's lap. Dolls could represent the two brothers.
- If you use different toys, change the words.

Something to Think About

This book shows people from a Native Alaskan Inuit culture. Notice with interest the items that are different from your home. "Look at that doll. It looks pretty." "See the boots the mommy is wearing? Those are called 'mukluks.' They keep her feet warm and cozy." "Michael's blanket is made of fur. I bet it's soft and warm." Point out that although these things may be a little different from what the children have in their own homes, one thing is certainly the same—how mothers and children love each other and like to snuggle.

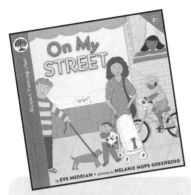

On My Street

by Eve Merriam, illustrated by Melanie Hope Greenberg

Story Synopsis

This story is a walk in a bustling neighborhood filled with a multicultural mix of people doing many different things, from washing cars to jumping rope and roller-skating. The neighborhood in the story is like many neighborhoods in any large city.

Reading Hints

Each page of the story is filled with many visual treats and a two-line rhyme that describes the person and what they are doing. It is a long "walk" for a young toddler so it might be a book that you would want to read at two sittings. Be aware of the children's interest and stop before they get tired.

Story S-t-r-e-t-c-h-e-r: Language

Who Lives on Your Street?

Materials
pictures from magazines
scissors
construction paper
glue

- Talk with one child or a small group of children about who lives on their street, in their neighborhood, or at their place of worship. Choose a location that is familiar to the toddlers.
- Talk about people's names and other common places that are found in most neighborhoods.
- Have a few large pictures you have cut from magazines and glued on construction paper of common neighborhood scenes. These will be helpful if the children are not very familiar with their neighborhoods or streets.
- Share the pictures with the children and let them identify what is going on.
- Put the pictures up for them to see after you have finished the discussion.

"Hope with a Jump Rope"

Materials
marker and large piece of paper

- Select two or three people that the children mentioned in the previous s-t-r-e-t-c-h-e-r discussion and help them make a rhyme about them.
- Print the rhymes on a large piece of chart paper and hang it on the wall for the children to see.

A Walk in the Neighborhood

Materials
camera

- Go for a neighborhood walk and take pictures of people doing things in the neighborhood, and shops and other services that are part of the neighborhood.
- Include the children in pictures that feature neighbors and popular gathering places throughout the neighborhood.
- Have the film developed and display the pictures for the children to see.
- If desired, make a book called, "Our Neighborhood".

Something to Think About

Displaying things for the children to see is very important. Displaying them at eye level usually means three feet from the floor. When reading to children who are sitting on the floor, the reader should sit in a very low chair or on the floor and hold the book facing the children.

Playtime: First Words, Rhymes and Actions

by Lucy Cousins, Anita Jeram, and Susan Meddaugh

and

Bedtime: First Words, Rhymes and Actions

by Lucy Cousins and Anita Jeram

Story Synopsis

Playtime and Bedtime are collections of well-illustrated rhymes and words about playtime and bedtime. Some of the rhymes included are "Hey Diddle, Diddle," "Wee Willie Winkie," "Goodnight, Goodnight," "Head and Shoulders, Knees and Toes," and "What Do Babies Play With?" All can be enjoyed anytime.

Reading Hints

Toddlers will enjoy flipping through these books and choosing a rhyme for you to read. The illustrations make the rhymes easily recognizable. It is not necessary to read these books from front to back as in a storybook. As the rhymes become familiar, toddlers will request specific ones and begin learning to repeat them with you as you read.

Story S-t-r-e-t-c-h-e-r: Movement and Music

Head and Shoulders, Knees and Toes

Materials
no special materials needed

- This is a very popular rhyming song with toddlers.
- Repeat the rhyme and do the motions of touching each body part as you say it.
- When the children have learned the rhyme and motions, it's time to add the music.
- This song is so much fun that you may want to sing it every day for months to come. It is truly an all-time favorite and one that encourages movement.

Toe Game

Materials
no special materials needed

- ■ "This Little Piggy Went to Market" is a classic counting game.
- ■ As you say the rhyme to one child, gently wiggle a different toe. When you get to the last toe, she will squeal with you "wee, wee, wee, all the way home."
- ■ Of course you must repeat the rhyme for the other foot and still, you will hear, "again, again."
- ■ It is truly a classic rhyme for the toddler set.

Acting Out "Hey, Diddle, Diddle"

Materials
paper
markers
tape

- ■ Draw a moon on a piece of paper.
- ■ Tape it to the floor.
- ■ Say the rhyme to the children.
- ■ Tell each child what part they will play.
- ■ The parts are the cat, the fiddle, the cow, the little dog, the dish, and the spoon. If there are more children than parts, assign two or more children to each part.
- ■ Say the rhyme again and encourage the children to act it out.

Something to Think About

Rhymes, rhymes, rhymes—the more you can read, the happier the children will be and the better prepared they will be for listening and reading. Having a collection of rhymes such as *Bedtime* and *Playtime* or *My Very First Mother Goose,* edited by Iona Opie, and illustrated by Rosemary Wells is a very good thing. When there isn't enough time for a story there's always time for a rhyme or two!

Pots and Pans

by Patricia Hubbell, illustrated by Diane deGroat

Story Synopsis

A little child has an absolutely wonderful time beating on pots and pans in the kitchen, accompanied by a cat and a puppy. The weary father, whose legs are seen in the background in some of the illustrations, shows up at the end with a resigned look on his face.

Reading Hints

As you read the book encourage the children to find the cat and puppy on each page. Stress the rhythm and the noise words as you read them.

Story S-t-r-e-t-c-h-e-r: Music

Pots and Pans Band

Materials

one or two pots, a wooden spoon, a couple pot lids, pie tins, or any other unbreakable kitchen thing that would make a good sound

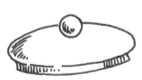

- Let the children make noise with the kitchen things after you have read the book to them. No instructions necessary!
- Add music later, if you wish.
- Join in the noise and music making!

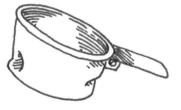

My Own Storage Cabinet

Materials
a low cabinet with a door, or a drawer
unbreakable things

- Designate one low cabinet or drawer for the children to use.
- In it put all kinds of unbreakable things they are allowed to take out and play with, such as old pots and lids, nesting plastic storage containers and lids, and old wooden spoons.
- Explain that this is a special drawer to hold things that they like to play with.

Pots and Pans in the Sandbox

Materials
old pots and lids
wooden spoon
outside sand play area

- Give the children pots and spoons to play with in the sand area.
- Model how to "stir" stones and sand, and other sand play.

Caution: Supervise closely so toddlers do not throw sand or get it in their eyes or their friends' eyes.

Something to Think About

Very young children love to play with pots and pans because they make a great noise, and the children are also imitating what they see adults doing. Young children need personal spaces that hold their "things." They also need to know that they are free to take things out and put things back in their space whenever they want. They derive a sense of security and confidence from having this space.

Roll Over! A Counting Song

by Merle Peek

Story Synopsis

Peek illustrates this childhood favorite song through the actions of a little boy who rolls over in his bed. Each time he rolls over, he imagines an animal falling out of the bed. By the end, he counts backwards from ten to one and all the animals are out of the bed. "Alone at last," he falls asleep. The comical blue and white illustrations are brought to life by the candle casting a yellow light in each scene.

Reading Hints

Count a child's fingers from one to ten, then count backwards from ten to one. Look at the cover of the book and ask the children what they see. Most will say that the monkey is falling out of the bed. Begin reading but do not sing the song, "Roll Over," simply read it. Read it again, and this time, sing the song. Soon the listeners will be singing along with you. Add the hand motions for rolling and counting.

Story S-t-r-e-t-c-h-e-r: Movement and Music

Learning the "Roll Over!" Song

Materials

no special materials needed

- Sing the song with the hand movements signifying the numbers and the rolling motion.
- Change the words of the song and instead of saying, "And the little one said, 'Roll Over,'" say, "And (Jeremy) said, 'Roll Over,'" inserting a child's name into the song.

Counting Different and Alike Things

Materials

blocks

puzzle pieces

small toy cars

- Using blocks that look alike, help one child or a small group of children count to five, or ten, if appropriate.
- Let the children put all the toy cars together, and then help them count the cars.
- Then place all the puzzle pieces together. Help the children count five (or ten) puzzle pieces.
- Encourage the children to play with the objects; point out number-related situations, "Sarah is playing with three toy cars," or "Jacob is stacking six blocks."

Roll Over, Teddy

Materials

nine stuffed animals and a doll

doll bed or pretend bed

- Place the doll in the middle of the bed.
- Line up the stuffed animals on both sides of the bed.
- Count the animals as you put them in the bed.
- Sing the song and when an animal falls out, let one child pretend the animal is falling out of the bed. At the end, whisper, "Alone at last."

Something to Think About

Learning to count by singing songs and counting objects is appropriate for young children, but do not expect that they know what "counting" means. They are learning the labels or the names for the amounts. Encourage them, but do not criticize them if they miss the order or cannot determine how many some group of objects represents.

Skip to My Lou

adapted and illustrated by Nadine Bernard Westcott

Story Synopsis

Humor abounds on every page of this book! It is silly, funny, and riotous. You can describe it any way you want, but this story is guaranteed to bring on laughs. All the work is done on the farm. Mother and father take the day off and go into town, leaving their son in charge. Things begin to happen and the entire farm is celebrating.

Reading Hints

Read this book slowly, pausing for the laughter to stop. It will stop because the children will want to see what happens on the next page. This is a sturdy board book, and small so the children need to be close to the reader to see the pictures.

Story S-t-r-e-t-c-h-e-r: Language

The Silliest Thing

Materials

no special materials needed

■ There is no doubt that this is a very silly story! There's no better way to describe it. All the things the animals do are preposterous and toddlers will be the first to notice this.
■ So after you have read it, talk with them about things that happen that are so funny they are just plain silly.
■ Ask them to share with you the silliest thing they ever saw or did.

Circle Dance

Materials

scarves
basket

- Put a few scarves in a basket.
- After the children learn to sing "Skip to My Lou," they should be ready to dance while they sing.
- Give each child a scarf.
- Let them dance around the room freely while you all sing the song.
- If you do not have scarves, hold hands and dance in a circle while you sing the song.

Learn "Skip to My Lou"

Materials

no special materials needed

- After you have read the book several times and the cadence of the rhyme is in everyone's head, you are ready to teach the children the music.
- If you have a recording of "Skip to my Lou" you could play it, otherwise just sing the song and the toddlers will join in.
- It is also fun to clap to the rhythm of the song.
- Sing it several times the first day they are learning it so they will know they have learned a new song and they will feel successful.

Something to Think About

Children do not usually skip before their fifth year. Skipping is not easy for young children, and is one of the later motor skills to be developed. Allow toddlers to do freeform movement and dancing without trying to teach them certain steps that they are not developmentally ready to do.

Ten, Nine, Eight

by Molly Bang

Story Synopsis

This Caldecott Honor book is the poem a father says to his little girl to get her ready for bed. It starts with "ten small toes all washed and warm," and continues counting backward to "six pale seashells hanging down" and finally, "one big girl all ready for bed." The text is printed on the left page and the brightly color illustrations have easy to spot focal points of illustrations that match the poem.

Reading Hints

Look at the picture on the front of the book and ask the children if they think the little girl is waking up or going to sleep. Let one child turn the pages of the board book. Look at the items in the picture, but call attention to items that are in both the print and the illustrations. Also, point out the numerals.

Story S-t-r-e-t-c-h-e-r: Movement and Music

Shoe, Shoe, Who Has the Shoe?

Materials
four pairs of shoes
lively recording of music

- Ask a small group of children to take off their shoes and sit in a circle.
- Show them the picture of the seven shoes in *Ten, Nine, Eight.*
- Line up the shoes, showing them that there are four pairs or eight shoes.
- Start the music and have the children close their eyes.
- While the music is playing, place one of the shoes on one child's foot and return to your chair, leaving seven shoes.
- Have the children open their eyes and count with you as you count the shoes—1, 2, 3, 4, 5, 6, 7.
- Look around for the eighth shoe and say, "Shoe, shoe, who has the shoe?" Wait for the children to notice who is wearing the shoe.
- Repeat the process putting the shoe on other children.

Magnetic Numerals

Materials

magnetic board or cookie sheet
toddler-safe magnetic numerals

■ Place the magnetic numerals out in a place where the children can manipulate them.
■ Read the book and each time a numeral is read, help one children find that numeral and place it in order on the magnetic board.
■ At the end of the book, let the children explore the numerals independently.

Seashell Pictures

Materials

seashells in various sizes
newspaper
masking tape
poster board
glue or glue sticks

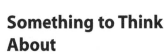

■ Let the children explore the collection of seashells, enjoying their textures, and how they are alike and different.
■ Have the children select six seashells, the same number as in the book.
■ Cover a table with newspaper and tape down the edges.
■ Have sheets of poster board or sturdy thick paper.
■ Provide glue or glue sticks and let the children glue six seashells onto the poster board take home with them.

Something to Think About

The enjoyment of *Ten, Nine, Eight* by Molly Bang is not to teach children to count backwards. It is the pleasure of counting and associating counting with a loving relationship. The father taking care of the child is also significant in the story. It is important to select books that show men as caring adults, as well as women.

This Is the Farmer
by Nancy Tafuri

Story Synopsis

The farmer's day begins when he kisses his wife. His day continues as his dog scratches a flea on the cat and the other animals greet the farmer as he makes his way around the farm. Watch for the mouse once he appears because he never leaves the story. Nancy Tafuri's large, colorful illustrations will delight young children.

Reading Hints

The illustrations in this book will give you a lot to talk about. Have the children find the various animals on each page. Talk about what they are doing and notice their facial expressions.

Story S-t-r-e-t-c-h-e-r: Language

Animal Collection

Materials
old magazines
scissors (adult only)
glue
index cards
clear contact paper
index card file box (optional)

- Let the children help you find pictures of other animals in old magazines.
- Cut them out (be sure scissors are not accessible to the children) and glue them to index cards. (Cover them with clear contact paper for more durability.)
- Talk about each animal. Describe how it looks—its color, what the fur is like, and other characteristics.
- Compare it to the animals in the book, if they are the same type of animal.
- As the collection grows, store the pictures in a card file box.
- The children will enjoy opening the box, dumping the cards out, and looking at the cards.

Story S-t-r-e-t-c-h-e-r: Movement

Hand Motions

Materials
no special materials needed

- Each page of the books invites an action.
- The children could kiss the picture of the wife, pat the dog on the next page, help the dog scratch a flea, or use their fingers to indicate walking directly on the pages of the book.

Story S-t-r-e-t-c-h-e-r: Movement

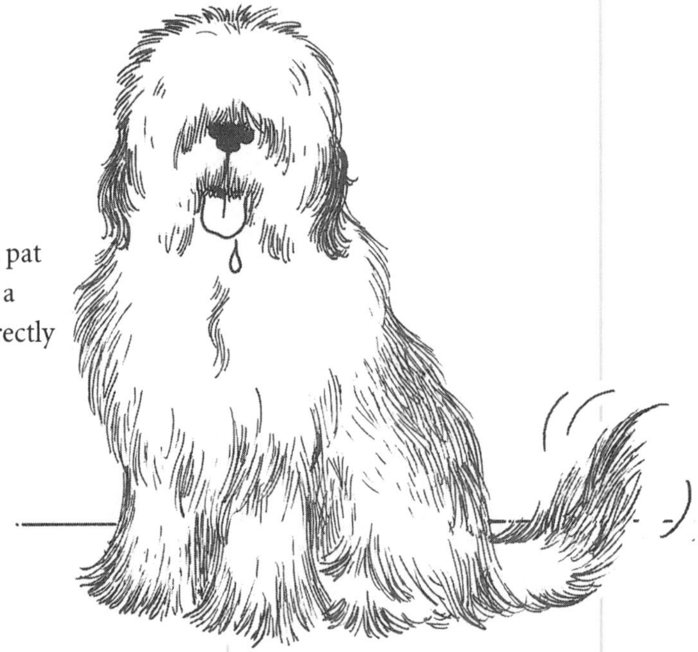

Act It Out

Materials
no special materials needed

- Once the children are familiar with the book, have them act out the motions on each page as you read the story. "Can you pretend to be the doggie and scratch the flea?" "Can you kick like the donkey?" "How does the farmer milk the cow?"

Something to Think About

Toddlers are fascinated by animals. When language is first developing, a child might point to a cow and say, "doggie," which to the child might mean, "four-legged animal." Expand the child's vocabulary by using the correct name. Toddlers delight in learning the names of many different animals and the sounds that go with the animals.

Tomie's Little Mother Goose

by Tomie dePaola

Story Synopsis

This is a charming book of Mother Goose rhymes for toddlers. DePaola's soft colorful illustrations will entice toddlers. This is a book to choose a rhyme or two and read it together.

Reading Hints

Select one rhyme or a few and snuggle up with a toddler or two. Read the rhymes and talk about the interesting illustrations. Keep this book close at hand for just the moment when you need a special treat.

Story S-t-r-e-t-c-h-e-r: Movement

"Ring-a-Ring O'Roses" Game

Materials

no special materials needed

■ Enjoy playing this game of holding hands and going around in circles while saying the rhyme.

■ The first verse tells the players to all fall down, and the next verse says to all get up again.

■ This will be a favorite toddler game.

Jumping

Materials

no special materials needed

- Read the two rhymes about "Little Jumping Joan" and "Jack Be Nimble."
- Read one of them again and encourage the children to jump along with the rhyme.
- Read the other rhyme and encourage the children to jump some more.

Story S-t-r-e-t-c-h-e-r: Pretending

Three Little Kittens

Materials

3 pairs of mittens or gloves

- This rhyme is fun to act out.
- Three toddlers can pretend to be the kittens.
- Explain that you will say the rhyme and they are to do what the rhyme tells them to do.
- In the first part of the rhyme they have lost their mittens.
- You will need to tell them ahead of time where to go to find their mittens when the verse says that they have found their mittens.

Something to Think About

Rhymes are treasures for young children. Whether the children are listening to them, chanting them, or pretending them, all these forms bring pleasure and new connections to the world of words and language.

Chapter 4—Books for Two-Year-Olds

Using Books with Two-Year-Olds

As their vocabulary grows and two-year-olds acquire more language skills, their thinking skills become more complex. Words become an anchor for ideas and thoughts. A two-year-old can enjoy books that follow a simple story line. Even if the image of the character looks slightly different on each page, children learn to keep the situation of the book in mind, a skill that is essential to developing concentration and making sense when reading stories on their own. Books like *All By Myself* by Ivan Bates is an example of a book that offers children this valuable practice.

This is also the age at which the beginnings of imagination emerge in children's play. Being able to understand ideas and talk generates a strong interest in pretend play. After reading an interesting book, twos love to act it out or imitate actions they saw in the book. They are translating what they see represented in pictures and words into real actions. They love to pretend to read! You might see a child "reading" a book to a doll or stuffed animal, as in the Helen Oxenbury book, *Tom and Pippo Read a Story*. They can even pretend to read a familiar book to friends, who are often an appreciative audience. Sometimes their imagination shows up in their fears. They have a greater capacity to think of the "what ifs?" They are struggling to be independent and yet still need a firm base of security. Many books address these fears and can help children gain confidence that life's difficulties can be handled. *The Kissing Hand* by Audrey Penn is a lovely example.

Of course, books expand a child's vocabulary. Reading to children reinforces words they already know; they also might also hear new descriptive words and learn their meaning from the context of the story. Emphasize interesting words as you read them and re-use them in your everyday talk. Books with a predictable pattern, such as *I Went Walking* by Sue Williams, are especially good for this age. It helps the children gain a feeling of mastery. Encourage the children to fill in the familiar phrases and guess what's on the next page.

Books can be an aid to friendship. Two-year-olds love being with other children. They make friends by making eye contact, smiling, and imitating each other. They love to be silly. Slapstick humor—running and falling down, making funny noises—is popular with this age, and is often reflected in their books. Although they love having friends, sharing is still very difficult for two-year-olds. That's one of the greatest things about books: They are easy to share! They were *designed* to share. Children learn that the pleasure in a book is enhanced when it is shared with a friend, so encourage children to bring books from home.

One of the greatest things about books: They are easy to share!

Techniques for Reading to Two-Year-Olds
- Ask the children questions about the text. Help them reflect on the ideas.
- Connect the events to children's lives. "Is that how you felt when you had to come inside?"
- Encourage children to "read" books to you.
- Make the story fit. Elaborate, eliminate, or otherwise change your reading or telling of a story if it improves it for the children.
- "Tell" a book when it's not convenient to read it. Do the children recognize it?
- Have a small library corner with comfy pillows, good light, and a bookshelf.
- Ask the wonderful question, "Do you want to read it again?"

Techniques for Reading to a Mixed-Age Group
Even with a mixed-age group of children with different language abilities, it is still possible to enjoy books together.

- Don't force participation. Simply sit down with a book and see who shows up. Others may join you as the story progresses.
- Simplify the text of a book, if necessary, so younger children can understand it.
- Let children take turns choosing the book.
- Older children can enjoy books designed for younger children. They might add comments.
- Ask questions that extend ideas, such as, "What do you think he was thinking about in this picture?"
- When you read a book geared to the interests of older children, have other books there for younger ones to handle.

Let children take turns choosing the books.

Books and S-t-r-e-t-c-h-e-r-s

All by Myself
by Ivan Bates

Story Synopsis

Maya is a little elephant who wants to get her own breakfast, but the tree is too tall. After trying many different ways to get the leaves from the tall tree, the mother elephant finds a way so Maya can do it almost all by herself.

Reading Hints

This is a great transition concept for children who wish they could do everything alone and want no help. There are many things young children can do with just a little help. This story will make children more comfortable about accepting help.

Story S-t-r-e-t-c-h-e-r: Language

Help Needed

Materials
no special materials needed

- Discuss the concept that it is okay to get help to do some things.
- Growing up takes a long time, many years in fact, and every day you learn new things you can do. Ask the children, "What are some things you need help with that some day you will be able to do alone?"
- Encourage the children that they will be able to do these things some day, and that until then it is okay to accept help.

Elephant Stories

Materials

a collection of several elephant photographs

- Collect photographs of elephants from animal magazines, from photographs on the Internet, or from pictures at a zoo.
- Share with the children a few simple facts about how elephants live, what they like to eat, and where they sleep.
- Invite any child to select one of the elephant pictures and to make up a pretend story about the elephant.
- Give every child who wishes a chance to tell an elephant story.

Breakfast Snack

Materials

fresh berries
mini-muffins
milk
bowls
glasses
napkins
spoons

- For a special treat, invite the children to have breakfast at school the next day.
- Have them help set the table and get things ready.
- Read the story and talk about breakfast and how important it is that we all eat breakfast every day, just as Maya and her mother did in the story.
- After reading the story, invite the children to join you at the table to share a bowl of fruit, a mini-muffin, and some milk.

Note: Check for allergies before serving food to children.

Something to Think About

It is very difficult to stop doing things for children, even when they no longer need help. It is amazing how self-sufficient toddlers and twos can become if we will let them. Before helping a child, ask yourself, "Can he do this alone, or with just a little help?"

At Preschool with Teddy Bear

by Jacqueline McQuade

Story Synopsis

Although he's a little nervous, young Teddy Bear enjoys his first day at preschool. He does many typical preschool activities, such as painting, building with blocks, listening to a story, and making a new friend.

Reading Hints

This is an ideal book to read at the beginning of the school year. Encourage the children to find similarities to their own life in the book. The children might even chant, "Just like me!" after each page.

Story S-t-r-e-t-c-h-e-r: Language

Photo Journal

Materials

camera
photo album book
small pieces of paper
marker or pen

- Make a photo record of the sequence of events of the children's day, from the time the children arrive until they leave. For example, daily events might include arriving in the morning, greeting friends, play time, circle time, outdoor time, lunch time, and getting coats on to go home.
- Let the children arrange the photos in order. Put them in a photo album.
- With the children, decide on the captions each picture should have.
- Write the captions, using their words, on small pieces of paper and put them with each photograph.
- Let the children "read" aloud the events of their day.

Play School

Materials

things from the classroom

- Suggest to the children that they play school.
- Ask them, "What do we need?"
- Let the children help you set the scene.
- Gather dolls and stuffed animals to represent the other children.
- If you take the role of a child, and a child becomes the teacher, see if he can lead songs or other rituals that take place at school.
- What other activities can he lead?
- Invite children to include getting ready to come to preschool in the morning in their role-playing. Have the children play the part of the adult—the parent—and you play the part of the child.

Story S-t-r-e-t-c-h-e-r: Sensory

Paint and Paste

Materials

smocks

paper

paste or glue

light cardboard objects such as
   toilet paper rolls, small box lids

tempera paint

brushes

- Look at the picture of the little bear painting.
- Say, "That looks like fun, doesn't it? Would you like to do that, too? Of course, we would never paint on our lap, would we? We need smocks. If you want to paint I'll set you up over here at the table."
- Show the children how to spread the glue or paste to make things stick.
- Let the glue construction dry.
- Then let the children paint the construction.

Something to Think About

Young children benefit greatly from having an adult as a pretend-play partner. Show the children how to set the scene and move the play along, but make sure you let the children take the lead. Whenever possible, involve other children as well.

Baby Talk

by Fred Hiatt, illustrated
by Mark Graham

Story Synopsis

Joey is at first mystified by his baby brother's cries and doesn't want to have much to do with him. That changes when the baby responds to his imitations of baby talk noises. The social bond develops as Joey learns to interpret his baby brother's baby talk to the adults in the family.

Reading Hints

Much of this story is a dialogue between Joey and one of his parents. They are talking about the new baby. When reading the dialogue, be sure to change voices for each person speaking. When reading the baby sounds, let the children help you say them.

Story S-t-r-e-t-c-h-e-r: Language

Baby Talk Circles

Materials

a baby

Note: Ask one of the parents who has a baby to visit the center on the day you read this story. Or, if there is an infant room in the center, arrange a visit with the babies in the center.

- First, listen together to the sounds the baby makes in a relaxed and alert state.
- Then show the children how to move closer to the baby and repeat the same sounds to the baby.
- Help the children notice how the baby makes eye contact and otherwise responds to the sounds the children make.
- Ask the children what they think the baby is saying.

Big Kid Abilities

Materials
chart paper
wide pen or marker

- Help the children make a list of all the things they can do that a baby cannot do.
- Talk about all the things that have changed, from the clothes they wear to the things they can now do.

THINGS I CAN DO.....	KIM	JANE	TOD
DRINK FROM A CUP	☆	☆	☆
DRESS MYSELF	☆	☆	☆
SING A SONG	☆	☆	☆
RUN FAST!	☆	☆	☆
SLEEP IN A BIG BED!	☆	☆	☆

Tape-Recorded Talk

Materials
tape recorder and blank tape

- Record the children when they are unaware of it.
- Let one child hear his own voice.
- See if he can identify other voices on the tape.
- Invite the child to talk into the tape recorder and play it back.
- Over a period of time, give each child a turn at talking into the tape recorder.

Something to Think About

The biggest insult to a two- or three-year-old is to be called a "baby." It is natural for children this age to enjoy adult comments that show they are no longer babies.

Backpack Baby
and Mine!
Backpack Baby Books
by Miriam Cohen

Story Synopsis
Backpack Baby and his father take lots of walks. In **Backpack Baby**, *the baby has a secret. He whispers his secret to everyone they meet on their walk. The secret is that his father, on his front, is carrying his new baby sister! In* **Mine!** *Backpack Baby shows the possessions that belong to him that he is carrying on his walk. In the end he is very happy to share with his father when his father asks for a bite of his pretzel.*

Reading Hints
Both books offer clear visual clues. In **Backpack Baby**, it is clear that the father is carrying something on his front. Listen for the children's comments about this. They may not have comments for the first reading, but subsequent readings will enhance the visual importance of the illustrations in these stories. Even though they are subtle, the children will pick up on what is going on, adding comments with each reading.

Story S-t-r-e-t-c-h-e-r: Language

Sharing Special Treasures

Material
paper bags

- Invite the children to bring something special from home that they would like to share with the other children.
- Explain that they will take their treasures back home at the end of the day.
- The next morning greet them with paper bags to put their treasures in so they will be a surprise to the other children, just like in the story.
- Let each children share their treasure in their own way.
- Use your judgment about whether they should be shared at one time, such as circle time, or spread out during the day.

Morning Walk

Materials

no special materials needed

- Take the children for a morning walk.
- If possible let them decide the direction they want to walk or the destination.
- Whenever possible, let children make the decision if there are several viable options.
- Talk about the people and things you see on your walk. Are any of them like what Backpack Baby saw on his walks?

Sharing Orange Snack

Materials
oranges
small plates
napkins

- Providing positive sharing experiences for young children is very worthwhile.
- Grasping the concept that sharing is fun contributes to the development of a positive self-image and turns tumultuous days into days filled with celebration and good cheer for two-year-olds.
- If you have read *Mine!* and you have a group of three children, use two oranges for the snack.
- Talk with them about the number of people, including yourself, who need a snack. If there are four people having a snack, use two medium-size oranges.
- Tell the children that you have two oranges and discuss ways to share the oranges.
- Peel the oranges and arrange the slices on a plate.
- Pass a napkin to each child and then pass the plate of orange slices, inviting each child to take one slice and pass the plate to the next person.

Something to Think About

It is easy for grownups to forget that young children are developing concepts for time and place. Any time beyond the moment or any place other than here is often difficult for them to grasp. Having no expectations for young children, other than here and now is the best assumption until you have observed them over a span of time and understand their abilities.

The Best Mouse Cookie

by Laura Numeroff, illustrated by Felicia Bond

Story Synopsis

*In this board book variation of **If You Give a Mouse a Cookie** Mouse is baking cookies. He falls asleep and they burn, but he simply starts over because you can never have too many cookies. In the end the best cookie is the one shared with a friend. The mouse is drawn in the same style as in the other books illustrated by Felicia Bond. He has become a childhood icon.*

Reading Hints

Show the children the cover of *The Best Mouse Cookie*. Ask them to predict what this book is about, who baked all of those cookies, and why they think that. Since the mouse has on a chef's hat, some children may already know that a chef's hat is associated with baking.

Story S-t-r-e-t-c-h-e-r: Object Play

Chocolate Chip Mouse Cookies

Materials
chocolate chip cookie dough
knife (adult use only)
cookie sheet
timer
oven (adult use only)
spatula
plates
napkins
milk

- Read the recipe for the chocolate chip cookies on the dough package. Follow the directions.
- Let the children help you place the cookies on the cookie sheet.
- Set the timer and let it go off so the children know the sound they are waiting to hear.
- Bake the cookies. Eat and enjoy the cookies.

Chef's Hat for Cookie Bakers

Materials
chef's hats
cookie sheets
oven mitts

- Collect chef's hats from restaurant supply stores or from parents who work in restaurants
- Let the children wear the hats while they play in the housekeeping corner or the kitchen area.
- Observe the play that evolves as they wear the chef's hats and the oven mitts.

Decorating Cookies

Materials
cookies
frosting, sprinkles, raisins
plates
spoons
plastic knives
milk
napkins

- Place the cookies and decorating materials on a low table.
- Put each decorating material on a separate plate.
- Let each child decorate at least two cookies for snack.
- Provide milk and sugar-free alternatives for those who can not have sugar or milk snacks.

Something to Think About

When young children are familiar with characters in a book and then they are introduced to a new book with the same character, they may find it confusing. Show the children *If You Give a Mouse a Cookie*. If many of the children already know the longer book, read it again, and then read the board book. Compare the two books. Twos will probably enjoy hearing you read the longer book, but they may prefer to explore the board book on their own.

Big Truck and Little Truck

by Jan Carr, illustrated by Ivan Bates

Story Synopsis

Big Truck and Little Truck work together on Farley's Farm. Big Fred and Little Fred drive these trucks. Big Truck has taught Little Truck everything he knows about taking produce from the fields to the market. One day Big Truck breaks down and has to be towed to the garage for a few days. Even though he misses Big Truck a lot, Little Truck does a valiant job all alone while Big Truck is away.

Reading Hints

The concepts of big and little are easy to understand in this farm story. Some of the vocabulary will be new to the children and can be explained as you read or tell the story. Tell the story the first few times and then expand it each time you tell it. Children are intrigued with trucks, and the red and yellow trucks in this story will become favorites for any child who hears the story.

Story S-t-r-e-t-c-h-e-r: Movement

Big and Little Walk

Materials
no special materials needed

■ Invite the children to go on a walk.
■ As you walk, identify things that are big and things that are little.

Big and Little Game

Materials

10 items (2 each, one big and one little of
    5 different items)
baskets

- Select a big and little toy, cup, box, stuffed animal, or
  any other object and mix them all up on the table.
- Invite the children to select all of the big ones and put
  them in one basket and all of the little objects and put them in
  another basket.

Visit a Farmer's Market

Materials

farmer's market

- Take the children
  on an outing to
  the local farmer's
  market.
- Look at the trucks
  that are there to
  see if they are big
  trucks or little
  trucks.
- Look at the
  vegetables and
  fruit. Identify big and little items.
- Select some fruit to take back to have for snack upon
  your return.
- If you do not have a local farmer's market visit a local
  grocery store.
- Call ahead and ask them to suggest a time for your visit.

Something to Think About

When you help children
understand the concepts of
big and *little*, be sure your
language and the activities
indicate a positive tone for
both big and little. Help
children develop non-
judgmental ideas that relate
to things that are big or
little.

Corduroy
by Don Freeman

Story Synopsis

Corduroy is an adventuresome toy bear who wanders around the department store at night. One night after closing the night watchman discovers Corduroy and puts him back in the toy display. Corduroy has lost the button from his overalls. The next day a little girl buys Corduroy. As soon as she is home, she sews on his missing button. Freeman's illustrations are expressive, classic children's illustrations. The bright red makes it memorable.

Reading Hints

Show the children the cover of *Corduroy*. Some may have already heard it or may own it. If they do, ask them not to tell anyone the story until you have finished reading it. Ask the children to tell you if they have a favorite stuffed animal and what the animal's name is. Explain that the little stuffed teddy bear in this book is named, "Corduroy." Help the children to say "Corduroy" several times.

Story S-t-r-e-t-c-h-e-r: Movement and Music

Button, Button, Who Has Corduroy's Button?

Materials
large cardboard button
recording of lively music
cassette player

- Play recorded music.
- Encourage the children to dance to the music.
- Put the large cardboard button in one child's hand while they are dancing.
- When the music stops, they all sit down and freeze.
- Then everyone shouts, "Button, Button, Who Has Corduroy's Button?"
- The one who has it returns it to the teacher. The game is played again and as the children dance, the teacher hides the button in another child's hand.

Story S-t-r-e-t-c-h-e-r: Pretending

Teddy Bears as Corduroy

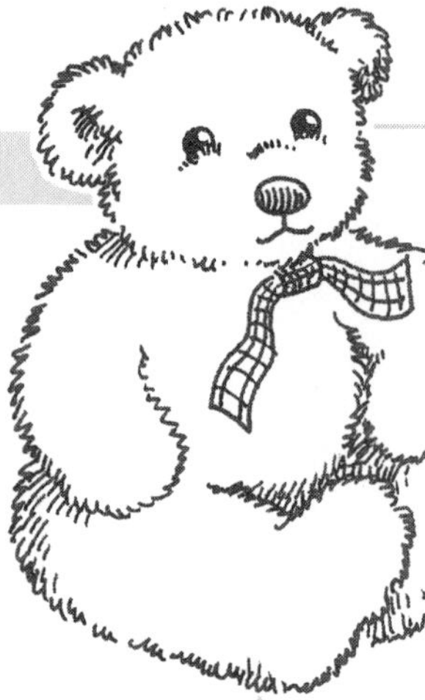

Materials

baby clothes or doll clothes to fit stuffed animals
teddy bears

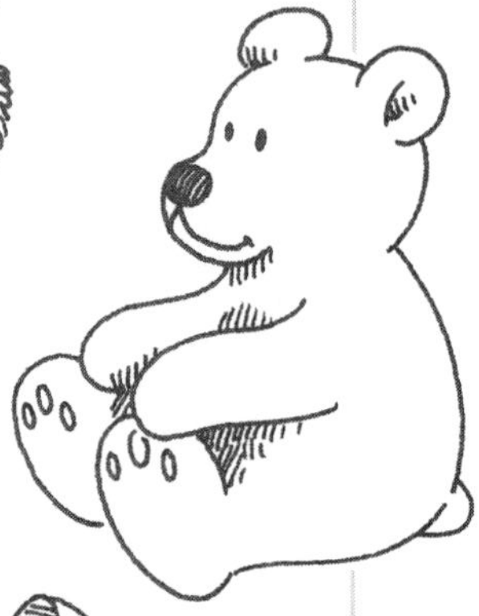

- Show the children some of the special clothes you have collected for their teddy bears.
- Help them find clothes that will fit their teddy bears.
- Let the children dress their teddy bears and when they are dressed called them "Corduroys."

Story S-t-r-e-t-c-h-e-r: Sensory

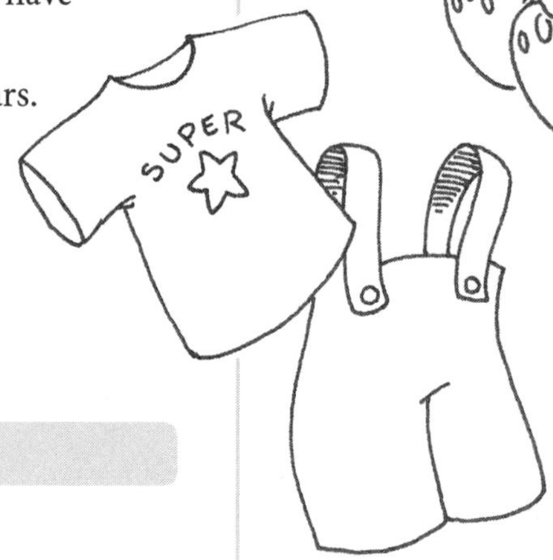

Button Pictures

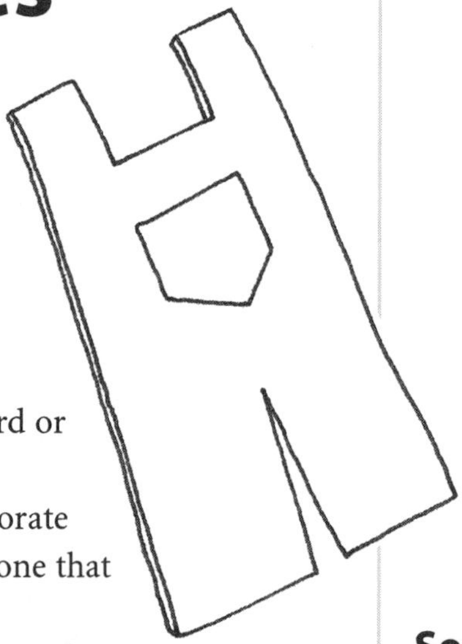

Materials

poster board or heavy construction paper
scissors (adult use only)
assorted buttons-large
glue or glue sticks

- Cut overall shapes from the poster board or heavy construction paper.
- Let the children glue on buttons to decorate Corduroy's overalls and to replace the one that is lost.

Note: This activity must be supervised at all times.

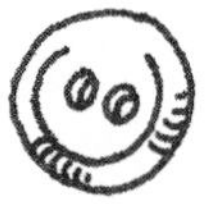

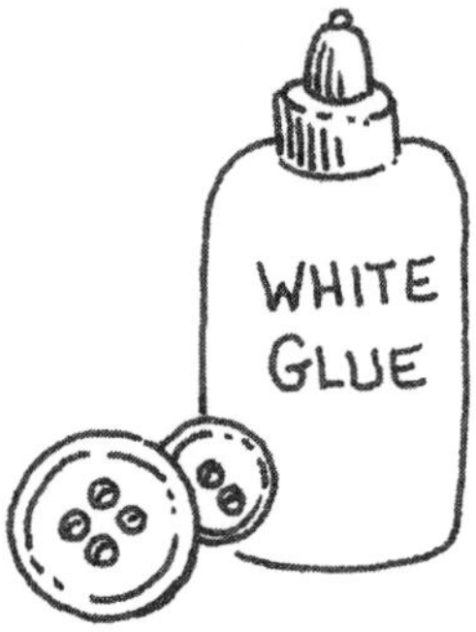

Something to Think About

Avoid letting children choose who will get the button in the game. Give out the button to make sure that all of the children have a chance to participate.

Each Peach Pear Plum

by Janet and Allan Ahlberg

Story Synopsis

This delightful book is written in rhyme and each scene is connected to the next through the narrative. For example, Tom Thumb is spied in the first scene, then his name is used in the second scene to relate to the next character in the illustration, Old Mother Hubbard. Each of the scenes contains a nursery rhyme or storybook character. The story ends with all of the characters at a picnic in the woods eating plum pie.

Reading Hints

Invite one child to sit on your lap to read this "I Spy" book with you. "Almost hidden" people are referred to throughout the narrative. Help the two-year-old see the characters if he does not spot them right away. You may have to point them out or give clues, "The three bears are going over the hill," or "We can only see Jack's and Jill's feet sticking up in the air." Since the book is rich in detail, children will enjoy reading and interacting with the pictures numerous times.

Story S-t-r-e-t-c-h-e-r: Movement and Music

Musical "I Spy"

Materials
cassette tape or CD of light instrumental music
tape or CD player

- Explain to the children how to play musical "I Spy."
- When the music begins, they can move around the room in any way they want to move—jump, march, or dance.
- When the music stops, they freeze, and stare at something straight in front of them. You will have to rehearse this part.
- Go to one child and whisper in his ear, "What do you spy?"
- The child whispers back to the teacher, "I spy Samantha's picture," or "I spy a clock."
- Some children will need you to help them with the "I Spy" clues.
- Say to the other children, "Jeremy spies something that Samantha made."
- The other children guess what it is.

I Feel

Materials

paper or cloth bag large enough to fit a child's hand
small toys

- Explain to the children that instead of playing "I Spy," you are going to play, "I Feel."
- Let them help you collect at least five objects, such as small toys, to place in the paper or cloth bag.
- Close the bag, then ask a child to reach in the bag, feel the object, and guess what it is without removing it.

Note: Be sure all objects are large enough to pass the choke tube test.

Hiding Pictures

Materials

construction or manila paper
crayons or markers or stickers

- Show the children how to create a hidden area by folding paper to bring both ends to the middle. This can be done horizontally or vertically.
- Open the paper and let the children draw or color on the inside. You can also incorporate a sticker of a favorite storybook character.
- Close the picture by refolding.
- Then let the children give you hints about what or who might be inside.
- Have one child open his hidden picture and share it with you and the other children.

Something to Think About

Young children like to repeat enjoyable experiences. For best results, use games such as "I Spy" and the "I Feel" bag several days in a row, changing only minor elements, such as having different toys in the bag.

From Head to Toe

by Eric Carle

Story Synopsis

A giraffe, a donkey, a seal, and other animals move their bodies and then they ask, "Can you do it?" The children respond positively with, "I can do it!" This is a perfect story to encourage movement and action.

Reading Hints

Read this story just as written and get ready for the children to move, move, and move! The children need to be on the floor or outside when you read the story. This will give them room to do the movements suggested in the story. It will be great fun!

Story S-t-r-e-t-c-h-e-r: Language and Movement

Can You Do It?

Materials

no special materials needed

- Read the story and invite the children to repeat the response and the action when you read about each animal.
- Be sure there is adequate space for active movements.

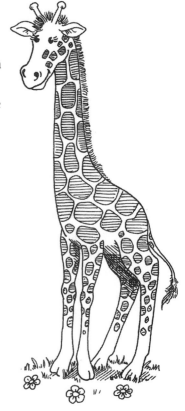

Sing "Head, Shoulders, Knees, and Toes"

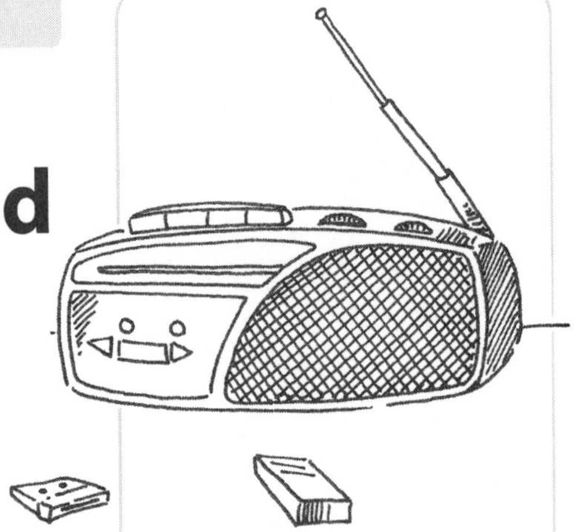

Materials
cassettes or CDs
tape or CD player

- In **Head to Toe,** Eric Carle writes about many different body parts.
- Singing "Head, Shoulders, Knees, and Toes" is a perfect follow-up to this story.
- Check your musical cassettes and CDs for a recording of the song.
- It is often included in collections of favorite songs for very young children.

"Guess Who?" Game

MEOW!

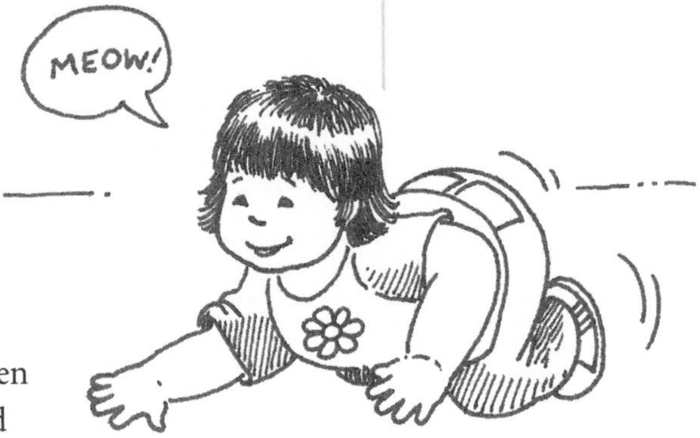

Materials
no special materials needed

- After you read the story, tell the children that they will have a chance to pretend they are one of the animals in the story.
- Let each child pretend to be one of the animals in the story and the other children can guess which animal they are.

Something to Think About

"Head, Shoulders, Knees, and Toes" is a great song to begin group time or to transition from one activity to another.

Hey, Little Baby!

by Nola Buck, illustrated by R.W. Alley

Story Synopsis

Big sister gives her baby brother and her mother explicit descriptions of all the things she is able to do. They are with her as she describes her accomplishments. She concludes her story by assuring her little brother that when he grows up she will teach him to do everything she can do now.

Reading Hints

This little girl has a healthy image of herself and her abilities. Read the story, which is told by the big sister, with confidence and appreciation of her strengths, as only she could recount them.

Story S-t-r-e-t-c-h-e-r: Language

Things I Can Do By Myself

Materials

no special materials needed

■ After you have read the story a second or third time, talk with the children about things they can do alone, and things they still need help with.

■ Encourage them to ask for help and to help each other when they are learning to do something and need a little help.

The "I Can" Game

Materials
ball

■ About halfway through the book, the little girl does very active things, including jumping, standing on her tippy-tip-toes, kicking the ball, and so on.

■ Take the book outside with the children and show them the pictures of these activities. Let them do these same movements and add some movements that they can do that were not in the book.

Story S-t-r-e-t-c-h-e-r: Object Play

Build a Tower

Materials
cardboard blocks

■ Building a tower like the little girl in the story will be a fun experience for young children.

■ Cardboard blocks that look like bricks are especially good building materials for young children.

■ These brick blocks are lightweight and are not a safety hazard when toppled.

■ If you don't have cardboard brick blocks you can make lightweight blocks from half-gallon milk cartons. Open the tops, rinse, and dry them first.

■ Tape the tops flat with masking tape and you have sturdy lightweight blocks.

Something to Think About

Every day, two-year-olds acquire new skills. Encourage independence whenever possible. Becoming self-sufficient in their daily routines is an important daily learning experience for young children.

A House Is a House for Me

by Mary Ann Hoberman, illustrated by Betty Fraser

Story Synopsis

A favorite among children and their teachers, this poem has scenes of insects, animals, people, and objects. Each stanza ends with the recurring phrase, "A house is a house for me." The language patterns and the cadence and rhythm of the poem make it enjoyable for young listeners.

Reading Hints

Let the children browse through the book and notice details in the illustrations. Begin reading the poem and teach them to join you in the recurring phrase. If sharing the book with a group of children, pause and teach them the recurring phrase so that all can join in. Read right through to the end of the book. Later place the book in a prominent spot where children may look at the illustrations independently.

Story S-t-r-e-t-c-h-e-r: Object Play

Building Block Houses

Materials
building blocks
poster board
markers
masking tape

- Encourage the children to build houses with blocks.
- Make a sign that reads, "Mimi's house," "or Josh's house," and so on.
- Tape the signs on the houses the children build.

My Play House

Materials

large box, such as a refrigerator or computer box
painting shirts
tempera paints and brushes

- Bring in a large box.
- The children will pretend that it is their house.
- Put painting shirts on the children and let them decorate the box with paints.

Getting Dressed and Parts of the Body

Materials

oversized hats, shoes, socks, gloves, coats

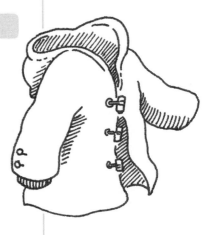

- Read again the part of the poem that begins, "A glove is a house for a hand."
- Let the children get dressed up in oversized clothes.
- After they are dressed, say, "A hat is a house for a head" and continue on through each piece of clothing.

Something to Think About

Long books may need to be broken up into two or more readings. Books that rhyme, such as *A House Is a House for Me*, move the action along because the children learn to predict the next rhyming pattern. If the book is too long and involved for the children, put it away and bring it out again in a few months.

Hug

by Jez Alborough

Story Synopsis

Most pages in this book have no words or use just one: "hug." A little monkey Bobo goes for a walk in the jungle and comes across many different mothers and baby animals, all giving each other hugs. When Bobo sees them hugging he says, "Hug." He feels very sad because his mother is not around to give him a hug. The other animals accompany him as he searches for her. He is just about to cry when he hears a familiar voice. The ending is surprising and special, not what you might imagine. Winner of the Oppenheim Toy Portfolio Best Book Award, and a Parenting Reading Magic Award.

Reading Hints

This book comes in two editions, a large hard cover and small board book. The board book is easy for little ones to hold and look at alone, and the illustrations are very clear. Children will appreciate hearing this story in your own words. For children who are talking, there are lots of questions to ask them, which they can answer from looking at the pictures.

Story S-t-r-e-t-c-h-e-r: Music

Two Little Monkeys

Materials
no special materials needed

■ Teach the children the words to the song "Two Little Monkeys."
   Two little monkeys
   Jumping on the bed,
   One fell off and bumped his head,
   Mother called the doctor and the doctor said,
   "No more monkeys jumping on the bed."

■ Learn more verses to this song in ***Where is Thumbkin?*** by Pam Schiller and Thomas Moore.

Hunt for Twos

Materials
small toys or other familiar items
bag

- Place small toys or items familiar to the children in a bag. You should have pairs of several items, some singles and three of a few items.
- Mix up the items in the bag.
- Let each child help you take an item out of the bag and put it on the table. Talk about what it is.
- When all the items are out on the table, ask the children to help you find two of the same things and place them side by side.
- Talk about the animals in the story and look at how many there are of each.
- Depending on the age of the children and whether they are ready, you may want to introduce the concept of a "pair."

Note: Be sure all objects are large enough to pass the choke tube test.

Pass the Hug

Materials
no special materials needed

- Sit or stand in a circle with the children and talk about hugging and how good it makes you feel when you give someone a hug.
- Start a hug with the child on your left and ask that child to pass the hug to the next person until the hug has gone all around the circle.
- When the hug has gone all around to the left pass another hug around to the right. This way each child will get to return the hug to the person who hugged him or her.

Something to Think About

This story is filled with important values and teaches children that animals might be different, but they all enjoy hugs. This concept is obvious in the story. You might want to enhance this concept while you're working with this story to help the children understand the beauty in diversity.

I Love You, Little One

by Nancy Tafuri

Story Synopsis

This beautiful poem about the love a mother has for her offspring shows tenderly drawn animals in beautiful natural settings. The repeated phrases and predictability of the text give children a sense of safety and comfort as the important message of love is emphasized over and over again.

Reading Hints

Once the children have heard the book a few times, pause and allow them to chime in on the repeated phrases. Give them a prompt: "What is the baby going to ask?" And on the last line of the mother's speech, you could say the first word, "forever..." and allow the children to fill in the rest. Eventually, reading the book could be almost like a comforting chant.

Mother and Baby Match-Up

Materials

pictures of animals, drawn or cut from magazines, catalogs, or calendars

scissors (adult use only)

cardboard

glue

clear contact paper or laminating machine

small pieces of felt

- Find pictures of baby animals and their mothers in magazines, catalogs, and calendars.
- Mount individual pictures on cardboard and cover them with clear contact paper or laminate for durability.
- Let the children match pictures of the baby animals with their mothers.
- Talk about the names of the animals as the children do this.
- Make this into a flannel board activity by gluing felt to the backs of the pictures.

Sandbox Worlds

Materials
sandbox
sand shovels
dishpan
water
grasses (cut off at base)
pinecones
small branches
small plastic animals

- Help the children make a model of woods and a pond in a sandbox.
- Dig a hole for the dishpan so the pond water will be level with the sand.
- Let the children stick grasses around the pond and put branches and pinecones into the sand to represent the woods.
- Help the children put the plastic animals into the woods and in the pond and play with them.

Note: This activity and any activity that involves water require extra supervision.

Nature Walk

Materials
volunteers to help on the walk

- Take the children for a nature walk, in the woods if possible. If there is a pond or meadow nearby, walk there. If not, nature can be found in a small patch of green, even in the middle of the city.
- Notice the sights, smells, and interesting textures you encounter.
- If you see an animal, stop and watch it quietly. If you see an animal home, such as a nest, observe it, pointing out that the animal needs its home.
- If desired, take photos of your walk and the things you see to enjoy and talk about later.

Something to Think About

Children learn respect for nature from the behavior of the important adults around them. Show them your awe of nature.

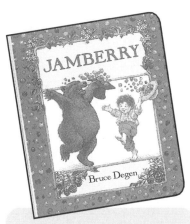

Jamberry
by Bruce Degen

Story Synopsis

Jamberry is a lively verse about a boy and a bear who celebrate finding blueberries, strawberries, blackberries, and raspberries. The rhyme and illustrations delight young children. After a few times reading this book, the children will begin to finish the rhymes and sing the chants, such as, "One berry, two berry, pick me a blueberry." The children will love looking at Degen's slapstick illustrations. They will like finding the little details, such as a mouse eating toast and jam as it floats in a boat.

Reading Hints

Jamberry must be seen, heard, chanted, and danced. After getting the rhythm of the rhyme, read it with enthusiasm. After reading it through once, go back and read and pause for the children to enjoy each picture. Read it a third time and let the children join in to complete the rhymes.

Taping Ourselves Chanting Jamberry

Materials
cassette tape recorder and blank tape

- Read **Jamberry** aloud several times, and then invite the children to "read" along with you.
- Many will already know the words because of the rhythm and the rhyme of the story.
- Record you and the children reading the book together.
- Play the tape so the children can hear how they sound.

Berryland Marching Band

Materials
rhythm band instruments
recording of marching music
tape or CD player

- Read *Jamberry* and point out the "Berryland Marching Band."
- Give the children the rhythm instruments and let them explore playing them.
- Put on the marching music and march around the room in time to the music.
- Call yourself the Jamberry's Berryland Marching Band.

Berry Pictures

Materials
construction paper in berry colors of blue,
    purple, deep purple like blackberries, magenta,
    raspberry, strawberry red and deep pink
white and manila papers
crayons and markers in berry colors

- Talk about the colors in Bruce Degen's *Jamberry*.
- Point out the blueberries, blackberries, strawberries, and raspberries.
- Let the children try to match the colors of the construction paper, crayons, and markers to Bruce Degen's colors.
- Encourage the children to make their own Berry Pictures using any of the berry-colored materials you collected.

Something to Think About

Have a berry-tasting party and ask children which they like best: blueberries, strawberries, blackberries, or raspberries. During berry-picking season, visit a berry farm or a neighbor's garden to pick strawberries from the vine or blueberries, blackberries and raspberries from the bushes. Always obtain written permission from parents before going on an outing, and invite parents to join you.

Just Enough

by Teri Daniels, illustrated by Harley Jessup

Story Synopsis

A little boy moves through an exciting day of learning experiences. Using a rhythmic text and bold illustrations, the author recounts all the things the boy is old enough to do by himself, such as "old enough to feed the fish, the wiggle 'round squiggle down fish." He is pleased with his independence and delighted to celebrate his pleasure.

Story S-t-r-e-t-c-h-e-r: Language

Make a Rebus Chart

Materials

chart paper and crayons or markers

- Talk with the children about things that they can do alone.
- Make a list of things they can do.
- After the children have gone for the day, print their words on a chart. It is very important to use their exact words. Save space at the beginning of each item and draw a picture of the activity described on that line.
- The next day display the chart for them to see.
- They will be excited to see the pictures you have drawn and will relate those pictures to the words on the line.
- Hang the chart at their eye level.
- Refer to the chart over the next few days to reinforce their accomplishments.

Story S-t-r-e-t-c-h-e-r: Object Play

Build a Big House

Materials

unit blocks, or any building blocks

- In the story *Just Enough* the little boy builds a big house with unit blocks.
- Throughout the day let each child spread out in the block area and build something of their choosing.

Make Yeast Bread

Making bread is a gratifying experience for young children.

Materials

1 tablespoon yeast

1 ½ cups water

1 tablespoon honey

1 teaspoon salt

4 cups flour (whole wheat and/or white)

loaf pan

oven (adult use only)

butter and plates

- Making bread is a gratifying experience for young children. Their developmental level will determine how much they are able to do, but each child will be able to knead a piece of dough and make a ball with it. The end result will be that each child will feel the success that results from turning a bowl of flour into a delicious loaf of bread. This is not an independent activity, but, as the story goes, children are able to do "just enough" to know that they produced the loaf of bread.

Authors' note: Carol Petrash, who was a teacher at Acorn Hill Children's Center, used this recipe with two- and three-year-olds.

- Mix one tablespoon yeast, one and one-half cups water, and one tablespoon honey in a large bowl. Stir well. Let the mixture get bubbly.
- Add one teaspoon salt and the flour. Mix well with spoon.
- Give each child some dough to knead on a floured surface.
- Shape into rolls or put into two loaf pans and let rise for 15-20 minutes.
- Bake rolls at 425 for 12-15 minutes, bake loaves at 350° for 50-60 minutes.

Note: Supervise children carefully when the oven is in use.

- After the bread has cooled enough to cut you can give each child a slice with butter.
- Take pictures of this experience, from beginning to end and write a description of what is happening under each picture. This makes a wonderful book!

Something to Think About

When planning experiences with children don't be afraid to pursue a project that might at first sound difficult for them. When a child is interested he is capable of the tasks associated with that interest.

The Kissing Hand

by Audrey Penn, illustrated by Ruth E. Harper and Nancy M. Leak

Story Synopsis

Chester is reluctant to leave his mother and go off to kindergarten for the first time. His mother teaches Chester a very valuable lesson. The lesson is that they can be separated, but Chester will still carry her love for him to school or wherever he may go.

Reading Hints

If you have two raccoon puppets, let one be Chester and the other be Chester's mother. Read the story to yourself several times until you are well versed in the sequence of events and the special phrases and language. Practice telling the story with the puppets saying the dialogue. It is a very easy story to tell and is filled with sentiment and love between a mother and child.

Story S-t-r-e-t-c-h-e-r: Language

Toasty Warm Thoughts

Materials
no special materials needed

- In the story, the mother talks to Chester about the importance of remembering toasty warm thoughts when he is away from her at school.
- She tells him to not miss her and to feel reassured that everything is all right.
- Discuss with the children toasty warm thoughts that they might have that make them feel good when they are away from home.

Hand Kisses

Materials

no special materials needed

- Show the picture of the mother kissing Chester's hand and folding the fingers over the kiss. (Have children wash their hands before you do the hand kisses.)
- Select a child to give a hand kiss to and then let each child pass a hand kiss to you or another child.
- Suggest that the children tell this story at home to their mothers or other family members before they come to school tomorrow.
- Remind them that the love the kiss symbolizes stays with the person even after they wash their hands.

Cookies and Milk Snack

Materials

cookies

milk

glasses

napkins

- Things that are familiar are often the most comforting to children.
- Most children recognize cookies and milk as a special treat or a comfort food.
- Read the story again shortly before it is time for a snack.
- After reading the story, sit together around a table and share cookies and milk.
- Talk about foods the children like, that make them feel good when they eat them.

Note: Check for allergies and food preferences before serving any food to children.

Something to Think About

You may want to substitute fruit or cheese for the cookies if you are being careful not to give the children foods that have sugar. It is a good idea to check with parents about their preferences for snack foods. Keep a list of these handy for ready reference.

Kiss It Better

by Hiawyn Oram, illustrated by Frederic Joos

Story Synopsis

Little Bear has a series of minor injuries, which requires a kiss and Band-Aids to make them better, all of which are readily available from the very empathetic Big Bear. Little Bear returns the empathy later that day when Big Bear gets bad news. A very sweet and humorous story!

Reading Hints

Use extra sounds of sympathy as you read the book with the children. Make up your own words. "Oh, poor Little Bear. I bet that hurt." Read the funny parts in a humorous voice and the room will fill with laughter.

Story S-t-r-e-t-c-h-e-r: Language

Cheer Up

Materials

puppet or doll

- Make the puppet or doll cry.
- Say he is sad because something happened. (Make up a situation.)
- Ask the children, "How can you make him feel better?"
- See what the children think of. A hug? A special blanket? A kiss?
- Encouraging children's problem-solving skills in a play situation like this can increase their range of responses to real-life situation.

Fix the Hurt

Materials
doll or stuffed animal
red marker or pieces of red tape
bandages or cloth strips
cotton balls
small bottle of water to represent antiseptic

- All children like to play doctor and fix "hurts."
- Tell the children that a doll or stuffed animal has been hurt.
- Put a red mark or a piece of red tape on the doll's knee or elbow.
- Provide a selection of pretend props the children can use to fix the hurt.

Stick It On, Pull It Off

Materials
masking tape
scissors (adult use only)
paint
paintbrushes
paper

- Cut masking tape into short strips to represent Band-Aids.
- Stick pieces of tape to the edge of the table where the children are sitting.
- Let each child pick pieces of tape off the edge and stick them onto a piece of paper in a random design. (Optional: Draw a bear face on the paper, or cut the paper into a bear shape.)
- Invite the children to paint over the whole thing.
- When the paint is dry, let the children peel off the pieces of tape to reveal the negative space design underneath.

Something to Think About

Young children learn how to feel sympathy for the distress of others from the examples of the important adults in their lives. This book is a great example. Two-year-olds are becoming more and more aware of feelings, and of having friendships. You can point out that people can be hurt in their feelings.

Mama, Do You Love Me?

by Barbara Joosse, illustrated by Barbara Lavallee

Story Synopsis

"Mama, do you love me?" is the question an Inuit child asks her mother again and again. She wants to know how much her mama loves her. Would her mother still love her if she did something bad? What would Mama do if she ran away? The story is a collection of her questions and Mama's reassurances. Barbara Lavallee's illustrations are stylized drawings with lovely patterns and expressive movements.

Reading Hints

Show the children the cover of the book and talk about the mother and daughter, who are dressed alike and sitting in a canoe. Read the title, "Mama, Do You Love Me?" and point to the words written across the big moon. Let the children look through the book with you, pausing to ask questions and pointing to items on the page.

Story S-t-r-e-t-c-h-e-r: Language

"Mama, Do You Love Me?" Animals

Materials
book

- Read or browse through the illustrations of the book and let the children point to the animals in the pictures.
- Let the children use their own words for the names of the animals, then extend their labeling, saying the correct name. For example, the bird is a raven and the children will probably call the lemmings, mice.
- Help the children learn the names of the musk ox, walrus, whale, and polar bear.

Matching Prints

Materials
different fabric patterns with small prints
scissors (adult use only)
masking tape

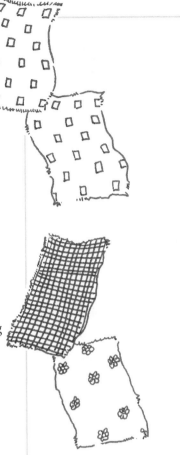

- Notice the different fabric patterns on the clothes the Mama and the little girl wear in **Mama, Do You Love Me?** They are usually small flowered prints with different colored backgrounds.
- Cut out two large matching fabric swatches of about 5" x 7" from each pattern.
- Turn them over to the reverse side and place strips of masking tape along the back to reinforce the edges.
- Show the children how to match one pattern, then let them play with the others creating matches by stacking the two matching ones on top of each other.

Water Play with Icebergs

Materials
water table or tub of water
ice cubes and frozen floats
different sized cups

- Pour a few inches of water into the water table.
- Float some ice cubes and frozen floats in the water.
- Let the children enjoy the icy water.
- After awhile, remove the ice and notice how the temperature changes.
Note: Supervise closely.

Something to Think About
"Mama, do you love me?" is a universal question asked by children. Numerous books for young children are based on this theme. The language and beautiful illustrations of the unfamiliar animals may be a challenge for some two-year-olds. However, the intriguing questions about mothers and their affections will get the attention of most children.

Marc Brown's Favorite Hand Rhymes
by Marc Brown

Story Synopsis
*Young children will enjoy the eight hand games and fingerplays illustrated by Marc Brown for the board book version of **Hand Rhymes**. Illustrations of the motions accompany each rhyme. Many of the familiar childhood rhymes are included, such as "Five Little Pigs," "Eensy, Weensy, Spider," "The Wheels on the Bus," and "Where Is Thumbkin?" The directions are easy to follow. The illustrations are colorful and enchanting accompaniments.*

Reading Hints
Select one of the hand rhymes that is familiar to you or the children. Read it from the book, then sing or chant it and do the motions. Select another one that is unfamiliar and sing or chant it and do the motions. Let the children select another one that they would like to learn.

Flannel Board of "Little Bunny" Hand Rhyme

Materials
flannel board
felt pieces for the bunny, squirrel, tree, duck

- Teach the children the chant and the hand rhymes.
- Echo chant each line until the children know each one.
- Let the children add the flannel board pieces to the flannel board for each animal Little Bunny meets.

"The Wheels on the Bus"

Materials

drawing paper or chart tablet

marker

- Draw a large picture of a bus without the wheels.
- Sing the song, "The Wheels on the Bus" and with each verse add the subject of the verse. For example, draw the bus without the wheels and as the children sing about the wheels on the bus, add them to your picture.
- Draw the children, the mothers, and the bus driver.
- Place the picture you have drawn in a prominent spot.
- Sing the song again, teaching the children all of the motions.

Kitten Sponge Painting

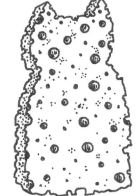

Materials

sponges

scissors (adult use only)

tempera paints

bowls

construction paper

- Cut sponges in the shape of a cat or a cat's paw.
- Pour a small amount of paint into the bowls.
- Let the children dip a sponge in the paint then press it onto their paper to create a picture or a pattern.
- Sing "Five Little Kittens" while the children are sponge painting.

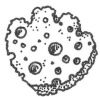

Draw a large picture of a bus without wheels.

Something to Think About

The children may know these hand rhymes and fingerplays with slightly different variations. For example, your children may know the spider song as "The Itsy, Bitsy Spider," instead of Marc Brown's "The Eensy, Weensy Spider." There are several different versions of "The Wheels on the Bus." Some add verses about the windshield wipers going "swish, swish, swish" and the horn on the bus going "honk, honk, honk." Still other versions have the horn on the bus going "beep, beep, beep." Sing whatever version the children know, then teach them Marc Brown's version.

Max's First Word and Max's New Suit

by Rosemary Wells

Story Synopsis

*There are eight Max board books. We selected two: **Max's First Word** and **Max's New Suit**. The stories involve Max and his older sister Ruby who takes care of him. Sometimes Max does things that cause Ruby much consternation and other times he is a wonderful little brother rabbit. Their facial expressions are filled with a variety of feelings for each other.*

Reading Hints

Sometimes telling the *Max* stories is the best way to present them. The stories often portray multiple feelings and actions that can be told better than read. There are funny little visual clues the children will identify and want to talk about as you move through the stories.

Story S-t-r-e-t-c-h-e-r: Language

Dressing (*Max's New Suit*)

Materials

no special materials needed

- Max clearly doesn't want Ruby to dress him.
- Talk about dressing for school and the different ways the children go about dressing.
- Let each child contribute to the discussion and encourage him to work on learning to dress by himself, if he is not already doing it.

I See It!

Materials
apple
egg (hardboiled or plastic)
broom
pot
cup
paper

■ Collect all the materials and put them on the floor where the children are gathered for the story.

■ Talk about each item and let the children name the items.

■ Read the story one page at a time, keeping the other page covered with a piece of paper so the children can focus on the object on just one page.

■ Let the children take turns identifying and holding up the real object that matches the object on the page.

Eating Apple Rings (*Max's First Word*)

Materials
napkins
apples
knife (adult use only)

■ Max delights in eating the apple and the story leaves no doubt that apples are good.

■ Have an apple snack with the children while you talk about the story and about apples.

■ Cut round horizontal slices and show the children the star pattern inside the apple.

Something to Think About

Learning that is fun is significant and lasting. If humor can be added to the learning experience it is even more valuable and more likely to be remembered. Using humor when negotiating differences between children often settles the dispute.

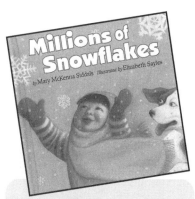

Millions of Snowflakes

by Mary McKenna Siddals,
illustrated by Elizabeth Sayles

Story Synopsis

A little girl is experiencing the joys of snow in winter. The rhyming verse describes the fun she is having as the snow falls around her and on her. The soft shades of pink and blue are wonderful colors for this rollicking tale of a two-year-old playing with her dog and the snowflakes.

Reading Hints

Reading this story on a snowy day in front of a window would be a delightful setting. The story rhymes are simple and easy for young children to recite with you on the second reading. Memorizing the rhyme will be easy for most children after only a few times hearing it read aloud.

Story S-t-r-e-t-c-h-e-r: Language and Movement

Snowflake Clapping

Materials
no special materials needed

■ The cadence of this rhyme makes it an excellent rhyme to clap as the children are learning the words.
■ Clap for each syllable in an even rhythm.
■ Most of the phrases will need four or five claps.
■ When you have a phrase with more syllables, make up a simple pattern that the children will pick up easily.
■ After they have the words memorized, let one child say a phrase and so on until the story is told.
■ Replace the clapping with tapping feet for even more fun.

Story S-t-r-e-t-c-h-e-r: Pretending

Dancing Snowflakes

Materials
silky chiffon scarves
waltz tape
tape player

- Give each child a scarf and go into a section of the room that is large and open where the children can pretend they are snowflakes whirling and falling as the music is played.
- Check the dance area to be sure it is safe for the children to move about freely and fall to the floor like snowflakes. If you have a carpeted area, use it for the dancing.
- Play the music and let the children move the scarves as they dance.

Play the music and let the children move the scarves as they dance.

Story S-t-r-e-t-c-h-e-r: Sensory

Catching Snowflakes

Materials
snowy day

- Bundle up with coats, hats, gloves, and boots if the snow is deep.
- Take the children outside and let them twirl and jump and hop around while catching snowflakes on the end of their nose.
- Let them do all the things the little girl does in the story.

Something to Think About
Playing outside every day regardless of the weather is very important for children. Be sure that the children have adequate coats, hats, boots, and rain gear for all kinds of weather. Send a note home or talk with parents individually about the importance of sending their children to school with appropriate outdoor clothing.

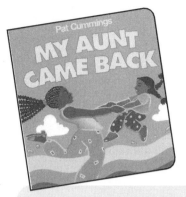

My Aunt Came Back

by Pat Cummings

Story Synopsis

In this book a beloved aunt returns again and again from exciting adventures, bringing the niece exotic presents. The illustrations show joy at their reunion and emotional connection. Finally, the niece is able to go along.

Reading Hints

A new exotic item is added on each page. See if the children can find objects in the new illustrations that have accumulated from earlier pages.

Story S-t-r-e-t-c-h-e-r: Language

Where Is It?

Materials

no special materials needed

- There are many exotic items in this book. When you first read it to the children, point to the object as you read it.
- In later readings, ask, "Where is the *quilted vest* (or other object)?"
- See if the children can point to it.
- When the children are very familiar with the book, give one child the closed book and name an object. See if he can find the object in the book.

Goodbye in Different Languages

Materials

no special materials needed

- Notice that the last page of the book has many ways of saying goodbye.
- Explain that people who live in different places have different ways of talking, and these are some of the ways people say goodbye.
- Help the children say these words.
- Use these words instead of your usual "bye-bye."
- Add new expressions to this list, such as "auf wiedersehen" ("goodbye" in German) and "adios" ("goodbye" in Spanish).

Adiós

Auf wiedersehen

Au revoir

Sayonara

Ciao

This Aunt Came Back

Materials

objects in the book: a wooden shoe; a vest; a fan; an umbrella; a ring; a beret (improvise if necessary) small suitcase

- After reading the book many times, suggest "you play it." Let a child be the aunt (or uncle) and give you the objects.
- Say, "Oh, my goodness, a quilted vest! Where on earth did you get that?" See if he can name the place from the book.
- For additional fun, brainstorm a whole new collection of objects that an aunt or uncle could bring back from a trip.

Something to Think About

Two-year-olds are learning that there are other places out there and that people come and go. Separation is an important issue for this age. The children will not understand concepts of geography and culture from seeing the book, but they will enjoy the wonderful sounds of names like Timbuktu and Katmandu. You are planting the seeds of awareness that the world is a diverse, exciting place.

My Own Big Bed

by Anna Grossnickle Hines,
illustrated by Mary Watson

Story Synopsis

The little girl in this story is a problem-solver. Faced with the exciting transition of sleeping in her own big bed for the first time, she imagines all the things that can happen. She could fall out, she might get lost, she might get lonely. But she comes up with a comforting thought: In a big bed, Mom and Dad can sit beside her to read a bedtime story and kiss her goodnight.

Reading Hints

Read this story with expression in your voice, sounding worried when the girl voices a possible problem. Then allow the children to use a very self-assured voice to repeat the phrase about being able to fix the problem.

Story S-t-r-e-t-c-h-e-r: Language

Puppet Fears

Materials
puppet or doll

- Have the puppet or doll come out and, with some embarrassment, say that he is afraid of the dark or of going to bed alone at night.
- Ask the children to give the puppet advice on ways to handle the situation.

Story S-t-r-e-t-c-h-e-r: Movement

Blanket Caves

Materials
several blankets
furniture, such as a table and small chairs

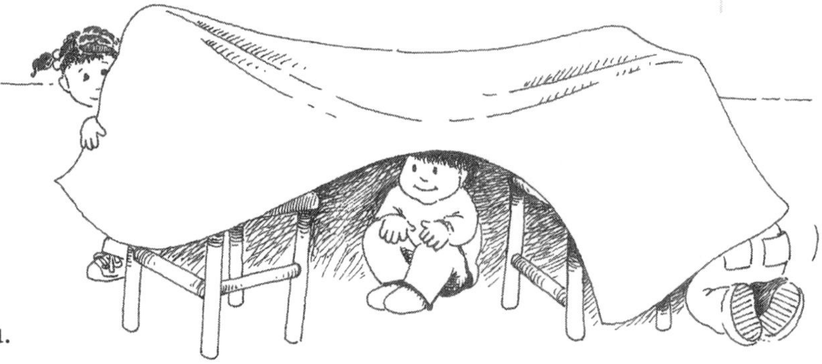

- Invite the children to make caves and tunnels using the blankets.
- Play with the children in these fun enclosures.
- Invite some stuffed animals to join you.

Story S-t-r-e-t-c-h-e-r: Music

Lullabies

Materials
doll or stuffed animal
recorded lullabies, optional

- Sing lullabies with the children.
- Talk about how lullabies are songs that make people feel calm and safe and help them fall asleep.
- Let a child pretend to tuck the doll in bed and sing it a reassuring lullaby.

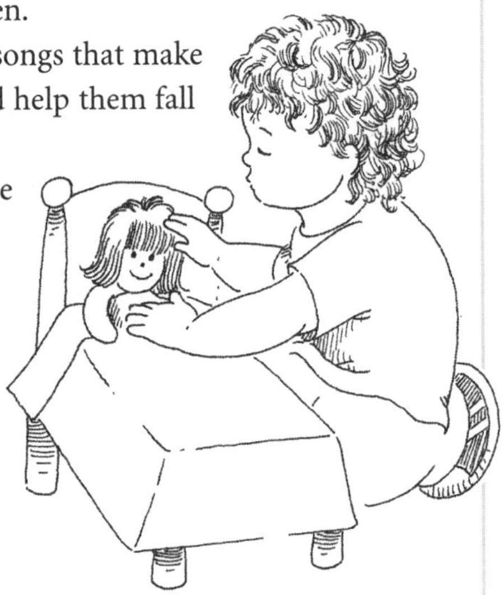

Something to Think About

It is common for children to have fears. This book has a reassuring quality that will help children overcome their fear of sleeping in a bed by themselves. Children are pleased when they overcome a fear like this by finding the solution themselves.

No No, Jo!
by Kate and Jim McMullan

Story Synopsis
Jo is the world's most helpful kitten. He helps Jen and Sam with everything they do. But they are not very appreciative of his help. On every double page there is a split page that folds back and reveals their admonition to the kitten.

Reading Hints
The children will be delighted every time you read this story. Suggest to them that they help you read the story in this way: Every time you open the split page you see the words, "No no, Jo." They should repeat this when you open the split page.

Story S-t-r-e-t-c-h-e-r: Language

Thank You

Materials
poster board
marker

- Print "Thank you" on the poster board.
- Set this thank you sign where all the children can see it.
- The story stresses the importance of saying "thank you." This is a good time to begin to practice using the words.
- Talk with the children about why we say "thank you" to others and when it is appropriate to say "thank you."
- One of them will notice the sign and "read" it, drawing the attention of the other children to the printed words.
- Leave the sign out for the children to reflect on throughout the next few days until they all know it.

Pet Shop Visit

Materials
pet shop

- Call your local pet shop to find a good time to bring the children to visit.
- Ask them about their kitten collection and when they will have several for the children to see.
- When you visit, be sure to talk about things that are important in the care of kittens and about being kind and gentle to them.

Playing with Toy Kittens

Materials
kitten stuffed animals

- Have some time when the children can play with the toy kittens after you have read the story to them.
- They will remember some of the things that Jo did in the story, and of course the refrain, "No no, Jo!"

Something to Think About

Most children are excited with stories that have repetitive refrains that they can say. If this is true with the children after you've read *No No, Jo!* several times, you might check out some stories or songs with similar refrains, such as the *Little Red Hen;* "*The Wheels on the Bus;*" *We're Going on a Bear Hunt; Chicka, Chicka, Boom, Boom; If You Were My Bunny; Jump Frog Jump;* and *Silly Sally.*

Pajama Time!
by Sandra Boynton

Story Synopsis

Boynton's black cover is punctuated with a cutout of a half-moon shape, bright yellow stars, and colorful cartoon animals dressed in pajamas. The book begins with an invitation to celebrate with a pajama time party when the moon is up. Many different pajamas appear, fuzzy, striped, and polka dotted, mismatched, red and green, and the ugliest ones ever seen. The rhythm of the language and the silliness of the illustrations have great appeal.

Reading Hints

Hold one child on your lap and let him explore the book first. The drawings are funny, and the child will turn the pages quickly to see the next fun illustration. Read the book with expression and excitement until the end, when you begin hushing your voice to almost a whisper, shushing and saying, "Good night."

Story S-t-r-e-t-c-h-e-r: Movement

Pajama Time Dance

Materials

pajamas

- Read the section of the book that shows the animals doing the Pajama Dance.
- Hold hands and shuffle your feet to a dance step while saying, "Pajammy to the left, pajammy to the right."
- Stand in place, put hands on knees, and say, "Jamma jamma jamma jamma." Then reach hands in the air and shout "P! J!"
- Walk around the room saying, "Now all around the room in one big line, wearing our pajamas and looking so fine. It's Pajama Time!"
- Do the dance several times and with each time, move slower and sing in quieter tones until the end is not a shout but a whispered, "p, j."

Matching Tops and Bottoms

Materials
several sets of pajama tops and bottoms
laundry basket

- Jumble up the pajama tops and bottoms like they might
  come tossed from the dryer.
- Ask the children to help you sort them by putting
  together the ones that match.
- Give younger twos fewer sets. Older children
  might have five or more.

Pajama Time

Materials
pajamas
toothbrush, one for each child
toothpaste
washcloth
blanket or quilt

- Lay out all the items children might need to get ready for bed.
- Talk about the pajamas the animals wore in the book and let
  one child select a favorite picture.
- Encourage him to pretend to do what the animal is doing.
- With the children, look at the pictures in the book and ask
  what the animals are doing, such as putting on pajamas,
  brushing teeth, doing the pajama time dance.
- Give a child one of the items listed above and ask him to
  pretend to use them.

Something to Think About

Create a naptime ritual to
help children rest. There are
many stories for young
children about bedtime,
naptime, and nighttime.
Find a collection of such
stories and read them on a
regular basis until the
children have selected their
favorite naptime books.

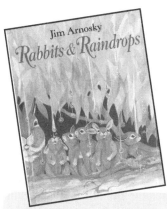

Rabbits & Raindrops
by Jim Arnosky

Story Synopsis

Mother rabbit takes her five baby rabbits out from under their hedge to enjoy the meadow. When it starts to rain, she rushes them back under the hedge. Other animals join them in that shelter.

Reading Hints

This beautifully illustrated story calls for a slow, careful reading. There is much to see and talk about on each page. The first reading should be told and not read so that you can talk with the children about what is happening to the little rabbits in the rain. Try alternating between telling and reading this story. The children will likely want to help with the telling after they get to know the story.

Story S-t-r-e-t-c-h-e-r: Movement

Pretend to Be Rabbits

Materials

no special materials needed

■ After reading the book, ask the children to show you how rabbits move. (It's helpful if they can first watch real rabbits.) Praise any movement they demonstrate.

■ Designate a place that is the rabbit's hedge "home," and move with the children to that spot.

■ Say, "Let's pretend to be rabbits and go out into the meadow." Describe how each little rabbit moves and plays.

■ Then make the noise of thunder and rain and shoo all of the children back into their hedge home.

What Is Waterproof?

Materials

water in a water table or dishpan
various items such as a small piece of fabric, a rubber shoe,
    a piece of fake fur, a plastic bag, and a sponge

- Let the children play randomly with the objects for a while.
- Sit alongside them and notice with the children how some things stay dry when water is under or over them, and how others absorb the water.
- Then talk about what a raincoat, boots, and umbrellas are made of and why.

Note: Supervise closely.

The World in a Puddle

Materials

a puddle

- After a rain, go outside with the children and find a puddle.
- With the children, look down into the puddle and notice all the things you can see, including a reflection of the world upside down!

Something to Think About

Children need to be outside every day. It is a good idea for each child to keep a rain slicker and boots at school so that there is never any reason to spend the whole day inside, even when it's raining.

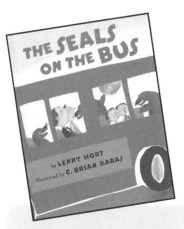

The Seals on the Bus

by Lenny Hort, illustrated by G. Brian Karas

Story Synopsis

All kinds of animals, including geese, seals, rabbits, monkeys, and skunks have boarded the bus. They all do whatever they do, and make the sounds they make. But the people on the bus need help as they travel all around the town with monkeys jumping and geese honking.

Reading Hints

This funny story is a spin-off of the ever-popular song about the wheels on the bus. Children will laugh loud and long with this story. You might want to read it just before playing outside, or, better yet, read it while you are outside.

Story S-t-r-e-t-c-h-e-r: Music

Sing "The Seals on the Bus"

Materials

no special materials needed

- The words in the story can be sung to the tune of "The Wheels on the Bus."
- If the children already know the tune you are ready to begin.
- If they do not know the music sing it one phrase at a time and let them join in after you have sung the tune.
- You may also find a cassette or CD of "The Wheels on the Bus" to play for them.

Animal Sounds

Materials

no special materials needed

- Show the pictures of each animal in the book and let the children identify the sound the animal makes.
- After the children have identified the sounds of the various animals, read the story again and ask them to make each animal's sound when you come to the appropriate page of the story.

Drawing Animals

Materials

drawing paper
crayons

- Gather the children around the table with their paper and crayons.
- Invite them to draw any of the animals while you read the story to them.
- Some children will be so involved in the story they won't be able to draw while you are reading. Give them time to draw when the story is over.

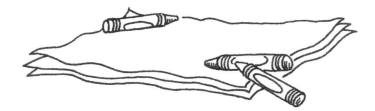

Something to Think About

Children who are reluctant listeners often enjoy a story more if they can sit at the table and draw while the story is being read. It helps them focus their attention. Cover the table with a large sheet of newsprint and put the crayon containers in the middle of the table. Let the children sit around the table and draw while you read the story.

Some Things Go Together

by Charlotte Zolotow,
illustrated by Ashley Wolff

Story Synopsis

This is a recitation of interesting objects and actions that "go together." Every few pages, the text reminds the reader that the adult and the child belong together too. This simple explanation of the concept of pairs is one that young children can appreciate and understand.

Reading Hints

There are many fun objects to point to and name in this book, many of which are not in the text. The children will enjoy finding them, and perhaps thinking of something they "go with."

Story S-t-r-e-t-c-h-e-r: Language

People's Stuff

Materials

objects or pictures of objects, associated with certain people

- Think of things that belong to or are associated with people or animals the children know, such as a briefcase for Mom, a lunchbox for brother, a dog dish for a dog, or a firefighter's hat for Dad.
- Show the children one object at a time and see if they can name who it belongs to or "goes with."
- If appropriate and safe, let the children play with the objects and pretend to be the other people.

Foods that Go Together

Materials
foods that go together, if desired
chart paper
marker

- When talking about familiar foods, ask what would go well with it. For example: pancakes and syrup, celery and cream cheese, cookies and milk, potatoes and gravy, or peanut butter and jelly.
- If desired, use chart paper and a marker to make an illustrated chart of these things.
- Serve some of these foods for snack.

Go-Together Collection

Materials
everyday objects

- Talk about other things that "go together." Possibilities include pots with lids, shoes with socks, toothbrush with toothpaste.
- Make a collection of these things.
- Mix up the objects and let the children sort them according to what goes with what.

Something to Think About

A two-year-old's vocabulary is growing to include words that describe actions and objects. This book enhances children's growing awareness of relationships. As the children become more independent, they also seek constant reassurance that the most important things that "go together" are the children and their cherished adults.

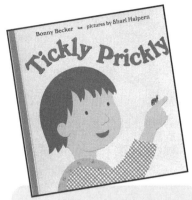

Tickly Prickly

by Bonny Becker, illustrated by Shari Halpern

Story Synopsis

Tickly Prickly *explores the way things feel and describes a variety of textures in rich, rhyming language. All of the things described in the story are found in nature, such as animals or insects. This book explores the sense of touch and a variety of things in our natural world that feel different.*

Reading Hints

Before reading the story, talk about the words *tickly* and *prickly* and see what the children think the story might be about. Find out what "tickly" and "prickly" mean to them. If they do not have any ideas about the correct meanings, explain their meanings and talk about things that are tickly and prickly. Also explore the ideas of "touch" and "feel" with them before reading the story.

Story S-t-r-e-t-c-h-e-r: Movement

Visit to Petting Zoo

Materials

no special materials needed

- Take the children to visit a petting zoo and let them feel how different each animal feels.
- If you don't have a petting zoo close by check with parents and others you know to find a family who has two or three family pets who would enjoy a visit from the children.
- Talk with the children about respecting animals, and taking care not to hurt them.
- Always stay with the children when they are in the company of animals.

Textured Picture

Materials

one piece of poster board or heavy construction paper
glue stick
4 to 6 different textured objects

- Make a textured picture with the children using objects with different textures such as a pinecone, a feather, a rock, and a seashell.
- Let the children help place the objects on a piece of poster board or heavy construction paper, using the glue stick to attach them to the paper. Help them leave enough room so you can write a word or two describing the texture of each object.
- Hang the picture at the children's eye level.

Touch-and-Feel Game

Materials

3 paper bags
3 textured objects, such as a hairbrush, suede shoe or purse, and a furry stuffed animal

- Have three paper bags with one object in each bag.
- Pass each bag around and let each of the children put their hand in the bag without looking inside and feel the object and describe in their own words the way the object feels.
- Use three objects that have very different textures.
- Use some of the children's words to develop rhyming descriptions of the object.
- Be sure to keep the activity short enough so the children do not get tired.

Something to Think About

Children need to be outside as much as possible. Collecting the objects for the textured picture is a perfect time to take a walk.

Toddler Two

by Anastasia Suen, illustrated by Winnie Cheon

Story Synopsis

Two happy toddlers discover that many body parts come in pairs. The story is an interactive adventure with flaps that reveal the body parts that are mentioned on that page of the story. The counting refrain "one, two" will delight youngsters as they learn that this is the proper response when the flaps are opened. Each time a flap is opened another pair of body parts is revealed.

Reading Hints

On each page of the story the children will see a pair of arms, legs, or other parts of their body. Let a child help you lift the flaps of the pages as you read the story. Tell the children that when the flaps are lifted they may count the number of parts they see. Each time you read the story let a different child lift the flaps. They will enjoy moving each different body part as you read about them.

Story S-t-r-e-t-c-h-e-r: Movement

A Hunt for Twos

Materials
no special materials needed

- Walk about the center or neighborhood looking for things that come in twos.
- It might be chairs, apples in a bowl, trees, flowers, and magazines.
- Two-year-olds will have fun with this game while developing a better understanding of the concept of two.

Story S-t-r-e-t-c-h-e-r: Movement and Sensory

Parade of Drums

Materials
round oatmeal boxes
hole punch or scissors (adult use only)
pieces of ribbon for drum strap
clear packing tape
2 spoons for drumsticks

- Make one hole on each side of the oatmeal box.
- The holes should be made about three or four inches down from the top of the box.
- Insert the ribbon on each side and make a knot inside the box.
- Tape the lid all the way around to keep the top secured.
- Now give each child two spoons and you are ready for a parade!

Tape the lid securely!

Two Colors Painting

Materials
painting paper
red and blue paint
brushes
easels or table
painting smocks or old shirts

- Mix the paint in advance and have everything ready at the easels or on the table.
- Talk about painting with two colors and remind the children where to put their brushes.
- Put painting smocks or old shirts on the children who will be painting.
- Remember that coordination will be different for each child. Be prepared for spills. The best way to help children learn about preventing spills and cleaning up is to let them help set up and clean up.
- As each child finishes painting print their name on their picture and hang it up to dry.
- Encourage the children to help with cleanup and to hang up their painting shirts.

Something to Think About

Round large brushes with fluffy bristles are very good to use with two-year-olds. Hanging the children's paintings at their eye level where they can see them will enhance their self-concept.

Tom and Pippo and the Bicycle and Tom and Pippo on the Beach

by Helen Oxenbury

Story Synopsis

The stories about Tom and his toy monkey, Pippo, are filled with expressions of feelings that are very familiar to young children. Children easily identify with Tom when Pippo falls off the back of his bicycle and when Tom wants Pippo to wear the "good" hat at the beach. These charming little stories are both written and illustrated by Helen Oxenbury, one of the most popular authors of children's books.

Reading Hints

Curl up on the floor on a rug or quilt and gather children closely so they can see the pictures in these little books. The stories are short so it might be fun to read two adventures in one day. Allow time between the readings of the two stories for children to have some active experiences.

Story S-t-r-e-t-c-h-e-r: Language and Movement

Animals on a Tricycle

Materials
tricycles
toy animals

■ Ask the children if they would like to take their animals for a ride on the tricycles.
■ Let them choose the animal they want to take.
■ Move to the area where the tricycles are located.
■ Help the children get the animals securely seated on the tricycle.
■ When they have finished with the rides talk about how they and their animal friends enjoyed the ride, and ask if they would like to do this again sometime.

On the Beach

Materials

newspaper

- Talk about the importance of keeping your head covered when you are out in the sun.
- Discuss the problem that Pippo had when he got to the beach and how the problem was solved.
- Tom's Dad took a piece of his newspaper and made a hat for Pippo.
- The children will be delighted to wear the paper hats and to help you make the paper hats. They won't be able to make them alone, but they can help.
- After the hats are complete, everyone can wear their hats outside.
- To document the children's involvement in this activity, take a photograph of the children in their newspaper hats.

Fold front flap down then turn over

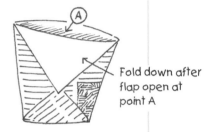

Fold down after flap open at point A

A hat for Pippo

Sand Play

Materials

sandbox or sand table
plastic pails and other plastic or other non-breakable sand toys

- Learning about sand and all the things it can do is a new experience for many two-year-olds, especially if they haven't been to a sandy beach.
- Explain the important things to remember when playing in sand and about sharing sand toys with friends.

Something to Think About

It is important that young children begin to develop their empathetic feelings. Having a favorite toy animal or doll that is with them in their play and that they want to care for is very appropriate for them, and a way for them to develop empathetic feelings for others. Keep handy a camera loaded with film. Making a photographic record of events throughout the year is a valuable tool for teachers.

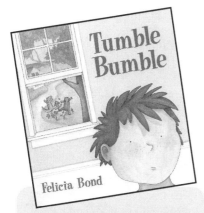

Tumble Bumble
by Felicia Bond

Story Synopsis

A tiny bug goes for a stroll, and meets a crocodile, a cat, a baby pig, and many other creatures. Each creature joins the bug on his walk. They finally stop to take a nap in a little boy's bed. When the little boy arrives he tumbles and bumbles with all ten of the animals. The animals and the little boy in this predictable story have a good time.

Reading Hint

Ask the children to keep track of the order in which the animals joined the walk. This is a good memory exercise.

Story S-t-r-e-t-c-h-e-r: Language

Name the Animals Game

Materials

no special materials needed

- Ask the children to name the animals in the story.
- Next name the order that each animal appeared in the story, first, second, and so on.

The Crocodile's Song

Materials

no special materials needed

- At one point in the story the crocodile tries to soothe the baby pig whose tail had been stepped on, and he sings him a song.
- Talk with the children about lullabies and other songs they like to hear when they aren't feeling well.
- Choose one or more of their favorite songs and ask them to sing one.

Dramatize the Story

Materials

poster board
markers
masking tape

- Print signs that name each animal in the story.
- The signs should attach to the children's shirts so other children can see the name of the animal they are pretending to be. Masking tape works well to attach the signs.
- Let each child pretend to be one of the animals in the story.
- Give them the name sign of the animal they choose.
- Read the story and let the children representing each animal pretend to take the walk as it does in the story.
- They will have fun with this while learning about sequencing and order.
- The tumble bumble part at the end of the story is especially fun to pretend.

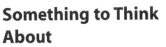

Talk with the children about lullabies and other songs they like to hear when they aren't feeling well.

Something to Think About

Children need routines in their daily lives. It is important for them to know that some things will happen every day. These secure feelings help children in their growth and development.

The Very Busy Spider

by Eric Carle

Story Synopsis

A little spider ignores the farm animals' requests to join them in their activities. The spider silently proceeds to spin her web of silky thread. The book ends with a lovely night scene and the owl calling, "Who built this beautiful web?" Eric Carle's illustrations are creative collages with raised lines that trace the spider's web. At the beginning of the book, there is just the outline of the web hanging from the fence post, but as each animal approaches the busy spider we see and feel the pattern of the web growing.

Reading Hints

This book should be experienced as a sensory, tactile experience as well as a visual experience. At the first reading, read it for the content and help the children follow the story, perhaps letting them point to the animals who come up to the spider. At the second reading, with one child sitting on your lap or beside you, have this child rub his hand over the web and feel the raised threads on the page. If the children feel the spider web during the first reading and begin paying attention to it, of course, encourage this exploration throughout the book.

Story S-t-r-e-t-c-h-e-r: Language

Silent Spider and Noisy Animals

Materials

no special materials needed

- Look at the pictures of the animals in the book.
- Help the children learn the sounds the different animals make. The horse says, "Neigh, Neigh." The cow says, "Moo, Moo," and so on.
- The children may not know the sound some animals make, such as the goat, "Maa, Maa."
- Show the pictures again and then read the book again letting the children make the animal sounds.

Walking the Spider Web

Materials
masking tape
scissors (adult use only)
cassette tape or CD of violin, flute, or harp music
cassette or CD player

- Create a huge spider web on the floor with masking tape strips.
- Talk about how the spider walked along the strings of her web.
- Start the music and have the children tiptoe or walk along the different threads of the masking tape web.
- When the music stops, they must stop, which can be a challenge for some children.
- Start the music again and the children start walking or moving along the web again.

Story S-t-r-e-t-c-h-e-r: Sensory

Our Spider Webs

Materials
lids or small bowls
thick white school glue
book
black construction paper
cotton swabs

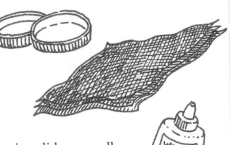

- Pour a small amount of glue into lids or small bowls.
- Feel the illustrations of the spider's web.
- Show the children how to dip their cotton swabs into the glue, and then paint it onto the paper.
- Allow the glue to dry and let the children feel how the glue is raised just like Eric Carle's spider web.
- As an alternative, put glue into squeeze bottles and let the children squeeze a string of glue onto the paper.
- When the glue dries it will be their webs.

Create a huge spider on the floor with masking tape strips.

Something to Think About
This valuable story should be read again and again to very young children. Early readings can focus on the tactile nature of the story, and later readings on the sounds the animals make and how the spider is quiet and very busy. Perhaps one of the most interesting aspects of the story is how all of the animals, who are so different from the spider, are kind to the spider: Each invites the spider to join them in their favorite activity. Sharing and celebrating differences are two of the special joys of life.

Chapter 5—Annotated List of Recommended Books

Aigner-Clark, Julie. 2002. ***Babies (Baby Einstein), Birds (Baby Einstein), Cats (Baby Einstein),*** and ***Dogs (Baby Einstein).*** New York: Hyperion Books for Children. These four chubby books are each about three and one-half inches square, perfect for little hands to hold. Each book is comprised of illustrations, photographs, and fine art paintings of the subject—a unique collection of little books, for baby's very first books to hold. (Board)

Bridwell, Norman. 2001. ***Clifford's Furry Friends.*** New York: Scholastic. Children can pet Clifford the Small Red Puppy and all his furry friends, the smooth cow, the downy duck, the fuzzy kitten, and more. The rhyming story and furry patches will delight all young animal lovers.

Brown, Margaret Wise. 1942. Illustrated by Clement Hurd. ***The Runaway Bunny.*** New York: HarperFestival. The classic story of the mother bunny and her little bunny playing a game of chase, and ending very happily. The story is 60 years old this year. The new Lap edition is a very large, sturdy board book. (Lap Board)

Christian, Cheryl. 2001. ***How Many?*** New York: Star Bright Books. Children will love discovering and counting how many little animals are hidden under each flap of this sturdy book. (Board)

Cousins, Lucy. 2000. ***Where Are Maisy's Friends?*** Cambridge: Candlewick Press. This is a funny game of hide-and-seek with Maisy and her friends. Lift the flap and find the friends. (Board)

1998. ***The Real Mother Goose Board Book.*** New York: Scholastic. A special collection of the best-loved rhymes from the classic edition in this sturdy book for the youngest child. (Board)

Frankel, Alona. 1979. ***Once Upon a Potty.*** New York: HarperFestival. This book is a great companion for a new potty and is sure to make the transition from diaper to potty more fun. There is one edition for boys and one for girls.

Hines, Anna Grossnickle. 1999. Illustrated by Thea Kliros. ***What Can You Do In the Rain? What Can You Do In the Wind? What Can You Do In the Snow?*** and ***What Can You Do In the Sun?*** New York: Greenwillow Books. These four books are excellent conversation starters with little ones. Each story begins with a question that can usually be answered with only one or two words with very lovely illustrations of a child doing something on each page that responds to the question that's the title of the book. (Board)

Hoban, Tana. 1993. ***Black on White.*** New York: Greenwillow Books. Black illustrations on white show objects such as a bib, a butterfly, a leaf, and keys, all with very clear contrast and easy to recognize. (Board)

Hoban, Tana. 1993. ***White on Black.*** New York: Greenwillow Books. This is the opposite of ***Black on White***, with white illustrations against a black background, such as boats, flowers, birds, and other clear illustrations of familiar things. (Board)

Hoban, Tana. 1994. ***What Is That?*** Greenwillow Books. Another high-contrast book illustrated with white on black that contains fun things to talk about with babies and identify in little games you can play while communicating with the baby. (Board)

Hurd, Thatcher. 1998. ***Zoom City.*** New York: HarperFestival. Filled with vehicles that make lots of noises, this book encourages something young children love to do—imitate the sounds. (Board)

Ford, Miela. 1999. *On My Own*. New York: Greenwillow Books. The roly-poly polar bear in this book is ready to play with his mother. Illustrated with excellent photographs.

Isadora, Rachel. 1985. *I Touch*. New York: Greenwillow Books. Babies love to discover their world by touching everything in it. In this story a very young child names the things she touches. (Board)

Leonard, Marcia. 2000. Photographs by Dorothy Handelman. *Splish, Splash!* New York: HarperFestival. This charming story is about a little girl who learns to stay dry in the rain with an umbrella.

Leonard, Marcia. 2000. Photographs by Dorothy Handelman. *Animal Talk*. New York: HarperFestival. A story just right for the youngest child who enjoys stuffed animals. The babies in this story play with toy animals and learn to make the sounds of each one.

Leonard, Marcia. 2000. Photographs by Dorothy Handelman. *Busy Babies*. New York: HarperFestival. These babies learn the joys that come from each accomplishment.

Leonard, Marcia. 2000. Photographs by Dorothy Handelman. *Food Is Fun!* New York: HarperFestival. A lively rhyme about food, from finger-licking Jell-O to yummy spaghetti.

Losordo, Stephen. 1998. Illustrated by Jane Conteh-Morgan. *Cow Moo Me*. New York: HarperFestival. Babies beginning to respond to rhythm and rhyme will adore the silly rhyming verse about all the animals and the sounds they make. (Board)

Melmed, Laura Krauss. 2002. Illustrated by Henri Sorensen. *I Love You as Much….*New York: HarperCollins. This beautiful book contains illustrations that could be categorized as fine art. It is a celebration of the love between mothers and children, a gentle picture-book lullaby. (Lap Board)

Miller, Margaret. 1998. Photographs by Margaret Miller. *I Can Help*. New York: Simon & Schuster Children's Publishing Division. A small square board book filled with colorful photographs of young children helping various family members doing work in their homes. (Board)

Miller, Margaret. 1998. Photographs by Margaret Miller. *Let's Pretend!* New York: Simon & Schuster Children's Publishing Division. A small square board book filled with colorful photographs of little children pretending to be everything from dinosaurs and astronauts to police officers and movie stars. (Board)

Miller, Margaret. 1996. Photographs by Margaret Miller. *Family Time*. New York: Simon & Schuster Children's Publishing Division. A small square board book filled with colorful photographs of small children engaged in activities with different members of their families. *Family Time* is filled with photographs of beautiful toddlers representing many ethnic groups. (Board)

Opie, Iona. Editor. 2001. Illustrated by Rosemary Wells. *Humpty Dumpty and the Other Rhymes (The Mother Goose Collection)*. Cambridge: Candlewick Press. There are eight favorite nursery rhymes in this little book—a perfect book for any time. (Board)

Oxenbury, Helen. 1981. *Working*. New York: Simon and Schuster Children's Publishing Division. Some other titles in the Helen Oxenbury Baby Board Book series are *Dressing*, *Family*, *Friends*, and *Playing*. They are perfect first books for babies to hold, with simple word labels and delightful pictures of babies. (Board)

Pinkney, Andrea and Brian. 1997. *Shake Shake Shake*. New York: Harcourt Brace & Company. The simple act of shaking becomes a fun experience for this toddler who is given a *shekere*, an African percussion instrument. (Board)

Rosen, Michael. 1989. Illustrated by Helen Oxenbury. *We're Going on a Bear Hunt*. New York: Simon and Schuster. A family story filled with delightful comedy and high drama. This is a tale of a brave family's joyous romp through sweeping landscapes. (Board)

Shaw, Nancy. 1997. Illustrated by Margot Apple. *Sheep in a Jeep*. Boston: Clarion Books. This hilarious story, told in rhyme, of a jeep filled with sheep going for a ride will have any child in stitches. Start with this one, and then read Nancy Shaw's other silly rhyming stores. (Board)

Simmons, Jane. 2002. *Daisy Says "Here We Go 'Round the Mulberry Bush"*. Boston: Little, Brown and Company. Join Daisy bouncing, flapping, hopping, and more on a delightful romp through the classic song "Here We Go 'Round the Mulberry Bush." The book is tabbed with a picture of a different animal on each tab. (Board)

Simmons, Jane. 2002. *Daisy Says "If You're Happy and You Know It"*. Boston: Little, Brown and Company. The book is tabbed with a picture of a different animal on each tab. Select an animal, and when you turn to that page, you see the animal singing the song, "If You're Happy and You Know It," and making the special sound that that particular animal makes. The *Daisy* books are excellent choices for the youngest child. (Board)

Stinson, Kathy. 1983. Illustrated by Robin Baird Lewis. *Big or Little?* Canada: Annick Press Ltd. On each page of this story the little boy describes something he does that makes him feel big or little. The superb illustrations make this a perfect book for a young child who is just beginning to explore the concept of his or her bigness.

Suen, Anastasia. 1998. Illustrated by Chih-Wei Chang. *Baby Born*. New York: Lee and Low Books. The activities of babies with their families take the reader through all the seasons of the year with a delightful rhyming story. (Board)

Sweet, Melissa. 2002. Adapted and illustrated by Melissa Sweet. *Fiddle-I-Fee*. Boston: Little Brown. A charming story of a little boy walking about the farm feeding all the animals and singing about each one of them. (Board)

Vulliamy, Clara. 1996. *Good Night, Baby!* Cambridge: Candlewick Press. The day is over and it's bedtime for baby. This book is a nice, cozy, quiet story for the end of the day. (Board)

Vulliamy, Clara. 1996. *Wide Awake!* Cambridge: Candlewick Press. The sun is up, and so is baby! Reading this story is a wonderful way to start the day.

Waddell, Martin W. 1992. Illustrated by Patrick Benson. *Owl Babies*. Massachusetts: Candlewick Press. The owl babies awaken to find their mother gone from home. This is a reassuring story that offers the promise that mommy will always come home. (Board)

Wardlaw, Lee. 1999. Illustrated by Julie Paschkis. *First Steps*. New York: HarperFestival. This rhyme expresses the feelings a toddler has who is just learning to walk. Both toddlers and parents can appreciate the excitement generated when a child takes those first steps.

Wells, Rosemary. 1997. *Read to Your Bunny*. New York: Scholastic. This story is an invitation to the world of reading. Children will ask to hear it again and again and soon they'll be reading it back to you.

Wellington, Monica. 1997. *Baby in a Car*. New York: Dutton Children's Books. A story about all the things the baby sees on one of his first rides down a busy street. (Board)

Indexes

Authors and Illustrators

Book Titles

Binding Index

Board Books

Materials Index

Title Information

PUBLISHER	TITLE	AUTHOR	ISBN
HarperCollins	All by Myself	Ivan Bates	0-06028585-0
David Bennett Books Limited	At Preschool with Teddy Bear	Jacqueline McQuade	0-8037-2394-6
HarperCollins	Baby Dance	Ann Taylor	0-694-01206-8
Simon & Schuster	Baby Faces	Margaret Miller	0-6898-1911-0
Simon & Schuster	Baby Talk	Fred Hiatt	0-6898-2146-8
Star Bright Books	Backpack Baby	Miriam Cohen	1-8877-3458-9
Workman	Barnyard Dance!	Sandra Boynton	0-5630-5442-6
Scholastic, Inc.	Bear Went Over the Mountain -Bunny Reads Back, The	Rosemary Wells	0-5900-291-0
Candlewick Press	Bedtime, First Words, Rhymes and Actions	Lucy Cousins	0-7636-0932-3
HarperCollins	Best Mouse Cookie, The	Laura Numeroff	0-694-01270-0
Scholastic, Inc.	Big Truck and little truck	Jan Carr	0-4390-7177-1
Henry Holt and Company	Brown Bear, Brown Bear, What Do You See?	Bill Martin, Jr.	0-8050-4790-5
Putnam	Clap Your Hands	Lorinda Bryan Cauley	0-399-22118-2
Penguin	Corduroy	Don Freeman	0-14-050173-8
Covent Garden Books Ltd. London	Diggers and Dumpers	SNAPSHOT Book	0-7894-1136-9
DK Publishing, Inc.	DK - Bathtime	N/A	N/A
DK Publishing, Inc.	DK - Colors	N/A	N/A
DK Publishing, Inc.	DK - Playtime	N/A	N/A
HarperCollins	Do You Know New?	Jean Marzollo	0-694-00870-2
Penguin	Each Peach Pear Plum	Janet and Allen Ahlberg	0-670-88278-0
Annick Press Ltd.	Families	Debbie Bailey	0-55037-594-6
Covent Garden Books Ltd. London	Fire Engine	SNAPSHOT Book	0-7894-1138-5
HarperCollins	From Head to Toe	Eric Carle	0-06-023515-2
Tupelo Books, NY	Have You Seen My Duckling?	Nancy Tafuri	0-6881-4899-9
Simon & Schuster	Helen Oxen. - All Fall Down	Helen Oxenbury	0-6898-1985-4
Simon & Schuster	Helen Oxen. - Clap Hands	Helen Oxenbury	0-6898-1984-6
Simon & Schuster	Helen Oxen. - Say Goodnight	Helen Oxenbury	0-6898-1987-0
Henry Holt and Company	Here Are My Hands	Bill Martin, Jr. & John Archambault	0-8050-5911-3
Workman	Hey! Wake Up!	Sandra Boynton	0-7611-1976-0
HarperCollins	Hey, Little Baby!	Nola Buck	0-694-01200-9
Viking	House Is a House for Me, A	Mary Ann Hoberman	0-6703-8016-4
HarperCollins	How a Baby Grows	Nola Buck	0-694-00873-7
Candlewick Press	Hug	Jez Alborough	0-7636-1576-5
Scholastic, Inc.	I Love You, Little One	Nancy Tafuri	0-4391-3746-2
HarperCollins	I See Me!	Pegi Deitz Shea	0-694-01278-5
Red Wagon Books - Harcourt Brace & Co.	I Went Walking	Sue Williams	0-1520-0771-7
Scholastic, Inc.	If You Were My Bunny	Kate McMullan	0-5903-412-6
Scholastic, Inc.	Itsy-Bitsy Spider -Bunny Reads Back, The	Rosemary Wells	0-5900-2911-8
HarperCollins	Jamberry	Bruce Degen	0-694-00651-3
Simon & Schuster	Jessie Bear, What Will You Wear?	Nancy White Carlstrom	0-0271-7350-X

PUBLISHER	TITLE	AUTHOR	ISBN
Viking	Just Enough	Teri Daniels	0-6708-8873-7
Dutton Children's Books	Kiss It Better	Hiawyn Oram	0-5254-6386-0
Child & Family Press	Kissing Hand, The	Audrey Penn	0-87868-585-5
Candlewick Press	Lucy Cousins - Country Animals	Lucy Cousins	0-7636-0609-X
Candlewick Press	Lucy Cousins - Farm Animals	Lucy Cousins	0-7636-0610-3
Candlewick Press	Lucy Cousins - Garden Animals	Lucy Cousins	0-7636-0611-1
Candlewick Press	Lucy Cousins - Pet Animals	Lucy Cousins	0-7636-0612-X
Chronicle	Mama, Do You Love Me?	Barbara M. Joosse	0-87701-759-0
Dutton Children's Books	Marc Brown's Favorite Hand Rhymes	Marc Brown	0-5254-5997-9
Dial Books for Yng. Readers - Div. of Penguin USA	Max's First Word	Rosemary Wells	0-8037-2269-9
Dial Books for Yng. Readers - Div. of Penguin USA	Max's New Suit	Rosemary Wells	0-8037-2270-2
Simon & Schuster	Me & My Bear	Margaret Miller	0-6898-2355-0
Clarion Books - Houghton Mifflin	Millions of Snowflakes	Mary McKenna Siddals	0-395-71531-8
Star Bright Books	Mine!	Miriam Cohen	1-8877-3459-7
Zero to Ten	More!	Sheilagh Noble	1-8408-9127-0
HarperCollins	My Aunt Came Back	Pat Cummings	0-694-01059-6
HarperCollins	My First Songs	Jane Manning	0-694-00983-0
Greenwillow - HarperCollins	My Friends	Nancy Tafuri	0-6880-7187-2
Greenwillow - HarperCollins	My Own Big Bed	Anna Grossnickle Hines	0-6881-5599-5
HarperCollins	No No, Jo!	Kate & Jim McMullan	0-694-00904-0
McGraw - Hill	On Mother's Lap	Ann Herbert Scott	0-618-05159-7
HarperCollins	On My Street	Eve Merriam	0-694-01258-0
Workman	Pajama Time!	Sandra Boynton	0-7611-1975-2
Candlewick Press	Pat A Cake	Tony Kenyon	0-7636-0431-3
Randon House	Pat the Bunny	Dorothy Kunhardt	0-3071-2000-7
Candlewick Press	Playtime, First Words, Rhymes and Actions	Lucy Cousins	0-7636-0933-1
HarperCollins	Pots & Pans	Particia Hubbell	0-6940-1072-3
Red Wagon Books - Harcourt Brace & Co.	Pretty Brown Face	Andrea & Brian Pinkney	0-1520-0643-5
Putnam	Rabbits & Raindrops	Jim Arnosky	0-3992-2635-4
Scholastic, Inc.	Rockin' Rhythm - Ring the Bells!	Billy Davis	0-4391-9263-3
Scholastic, Inc.	Rockin' Rhythm - Shake the Maracas!	Billy Davis	0-4391-9261-7
Scholastic, Inc.	Rockin' Rhythm - Tap the Tambourine!	Billy Davis	0-4391-9260-9
Clarion Books - Houghton Mifflin	Roll Over! A Counting Song	Merle Peek	0-3959-8037-2
DK Publishing, Inc.	Scratch & Sniff - Food	DK Books	0-7894-3988-3
DK Publishing, Inc.	Scratch & Sniff - Garden	DK Books	0-7894-3989-1
DK Publishing, Inc.	Scratch & Sniff - Party	DK Books	0-7894-5224-3
DK Publishing, Inc.	Scratch & Sniff - Shopping	DK Books	0-7894-5223-5
Henry Holt and Company	Seals on the Bus, The	Lenny Hort	0-8050-5952-0
HarperCollins	Show Me!	Tom Tracy	0-694-01039-1
Little, Brown and Company	Skip to My Lou	Nadine Bernard Westcott	0-316-93091-1
HarperCollins	Some Things Go Together	Charlotte Zolotow	0-694-01197-5
Putnam	Spot Books - Spot Goes to the Park	Eric Hill	0-3992-1833-5

PUBLISHER	TITLE	AUTHOR	ISBN
Putnam	Spot Books – Spot's Touch & Feel Day	Eric Hill	0-3992-3209-5
Putnam	Spot Books - Where's Spot	Eric Hill	0-3992-0258-9
Greenwillow - HarperCollins	Ten, Nine, Eight	Molly Bang	0-6881-4901-4
Red Wagon Books - Harcourt Brace & Co.	Things That Go - Plane	Chris L. Demarest	0-1520-0268-5
Red Wagon Books - Harcourt Brace & Co.	Things That Go - Ship	Chris L. Demarest	0-1520-0267-7
Red Wagon Books - Harcourt Brace & Co.	Things That Go- Bus	Chris L. Demarest	0-1520-0810-1
Red Wagon Books - Harcourt Brace & Co.	Things That Go -Train	Chris L. Demarest	0-1520-0809-8
Greenwillow - HarperCollins	This Is the Farmer	Nancy Tafuri	0-6880-9462-6
Little Simon	Tickle Tickle	Helen Oxenbury	0-689-81986-2
HarperCollins	Tickly Prickly	Bonny Becker	0-694-01239-4
Lee & Low Books Inc.	Toddler Two	Anastasia Suen	1-58430-015-9
Candlewick Press	Tom and Pippo and the Bicycle	Helen Oxenbury	0-7636-0162-4
Candlewick Press	Tom and Pippo on the Beach	Helen Oxenbury	0-7636-0163-2
Simon & Schuster	Tom and Pippo Read a Story	Helen Oxenbury	0-6898-1958-7
Putnam	Tomie's Little Mother Goose	Tomie dePaola	0-399-23154-4
DK Publishers, Inc	Touch & Feel - Clothes	Deni Brown	0-7894-2919-5
DK Publishers, Inc	Touch & Feel - Home	Deni Brown	0-7894-2917-9
DK Publishers, Inc	Touch & Feel - Kitten	Deni Brown	0-7894-3990-5
DK Publishers, Inc	Touch & Feel - Puppy	Deni Brown	0-7894-3991-3
HarperCollins	Tumble Bumble	Felicia Bond	0-06-443585-7
Zero to Ten	Uh Oh!	Sheilagh Noble	1-8408-9182-3
Philomel Books - Penguin Putnam	Very Busy Spider, The	Eric Carle	0-399-22919-1
Zero to Ten	Whoops!	Louise Batchelor	0-84089024-0
HarperCollins	Wrapping Paper Romp	Patricia Hubbell	0-694-01098-7
HarperCollins	You Are My Perfect Baby	Joyce Carol Thomas	0-694-01096-0

Games to Play with Babies, Third Edition

Jackie Silberg

Hundreds of games to play with your baby to encourage bonding, coordination, motor skills, and more! At last…the eagerly awaited new edition of one of the most trusted and popular books on infant development is here! Completely redesigned with 50 brand-new games and all new illustrations, this indispensable book shows you how to build important developmental skills while enjoying time with your baby. Use these everyday activities to nurture and stimulate self-confidence, coordination, social skills, and much, much more. Give your baby a great start with this wonderful collection of over 225 fun-filled games! 256 pages. 2001.

ISBN 0-87659-255-8 / Gryphon House / 16285 / PB

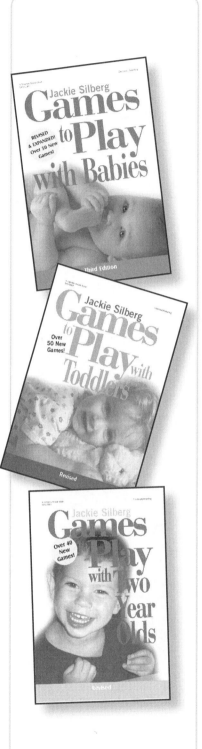

Games to Play with Toddlers, Revised

Jackie Silberg

Revised and updated with all new illustrations and over 200 games, this indispensable book helps you develop areas important for the growth of your 12- to 24-month-old—areas such as language, creativity, coordination, confidence, problem-solving, and gross motor skills. You and your toddler will experience the joy of discovery on every fun-filled page! 256 pages.

ISBN 0-87659-234-5 / Gryphon House / 19587 / PB

Games to Play with Two Year Olds, Revised

Jackie Silberg

Revised and updated, *Games to Play with Two Year Olds* is packed with opportunities to build confidence and to enhance language, coordination, social interactions, and problem-solving skills. *Games to Play with Two Year Olds* is a must-have for anyone caring for a child between the ages of two and three. Turn ordinary, everyday routines into fun learning experiences! 256 pages.

ISBN 0-87659-235-3 / Gryphon House / 12687 / PB

THE INNOVATIONS CURRICULUM

Kay Albrecht and Linda G. Miller

Everything you need for a complete infant and toddler program. The *Innovations* curriculum series is a comprehensive, interactive curriculum for infants and toddlers. Responding to children's interests is at the heart of emergent curriculum and central to the *Innovations* series, which meets a full spectrum of needs for teachers, parents, and the children they care for.

Innovations: The Comprehensive Infant Curriculum

416 pages. 2000.

ISBN 0-87659-213-2 / Gryphon House / 14962 / PB
• Early Childhood News Director's Award

Innovations: The Comprehensive Toddler Curriculum

416 pages. 2000.

ISBN 0-87659-214-0 / Gryphon House / 17846 / PB
• Early Childhood News Director's Award

Innovations: Infant and Toddler Development

Kay Albrecht and Linda G. Miller

This comprehensive resource provides teachers with a thorough understanding of the knowledge base that informs early childhood practice. Focusing on the development of children from birth to age three, *Innovations* gives you an in-depth guide to the underlying ages and stages, theories, and best practices of the early childhood field, so you can create opportunities for infants and toddlers to learn and teachers to teach.

Enhance interactions and classroom environment with wide-ranging understanding of infant and toddler development. Topics include:

- managing normal aggression
- theories of infant and toddler development
- best practices
- the development of language skills
- teaching social problem-solving
- guidance and discipline. 372 pages. 2001.

ISBN 0-87659-259-0 / Gryphon House / 19237 / PB

Available at your favorite bookstore, school supply store, or order from Gryphon House at 800.638.0928 or www.gryphonhouse.com.

First Art
Art Experiences for Toddlers and Twos
MaryAnn F. Kohl

Jump right in—doing art with toddlers and twos is fun, rewarding, and a wonderful learning experience. Children discover their world as they explore the 75 fun-filled art adventures in *First Art*. They will joyfully squeeze a rainbow, make their own (safe) beads to string, and create their very own painted paper quilt. *First Art* starts children on a journey full of exploration and creativity! 160 pages.

ISBN 0-87659-222-1 / Gryphon House / 18543 / PB

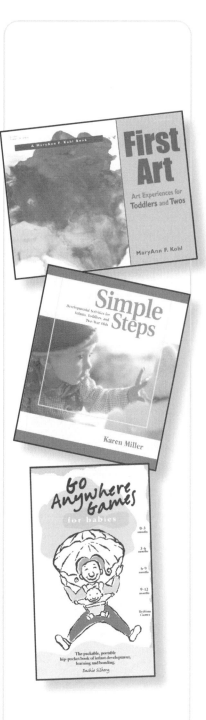

Simple Steps
Developmental Activities for Infants, Toddlers, and Two-Year-Olds
Karen Miller

Open the door to teaching infants, toddlers, and two-year-olds successfullly with these 300 activities linked to the recent research in child development. *Simple Steps* outlines a typical developmental sequence in ten areas: social/emotional, fine motor, gross motor, language, cognitive, sensory, nature, music and movement, creativity, and dramatic play. 296 pages. 1999.

ISBN 0-87659-204-3 / Gryphon House / 18274 / PB

Go Anywhere Games for Babies
Jackie Silberg

Have you ever needed just a little help when you were out with your baby? More than 60 fun games designed to play on the bus, in the waiting room, at the park, or right at home. Written by the best-selling baby game author Jackie Silberg, it's printed on extra-heavy coated paper for maximum durability, and uses a special binding that lies flat on any surface—even a parent's knee! Sections include games for babies birth to 3 months, 3-6 months, 6-9 months and 9-12 months, plus a bonus section of going-to-sleep games. 84 pages. 2000.

ISBN 1-58904-006-6 / Robins Lane Press /16925 / Wiro Spine

• Early Childhood News Director's Award

Available at your favorite bookstore, school supply store, or order from Gryphon House at 800.638.0928 or www.gryphonhouse.com.

Each Story S-t-r-e-t-c-h-e-r-s® features:

- 450 teaching ideas based on teacher-recommended books
- classroom-tested, developmentally sound learning discoveries
- ready-to-use activities based on 90 children's books
- 18 integrated, thematic units
- each children's book is s-t-r-e-t-c-h-e-d five ways with activities that heighten reading readiness and sharpen comprehension skills.

Story S-t-r-e-t-c-h-e-r-s®
Activities to Expand Children's Favorite Books (Pre-K–K)
Shirley C. Raines and Robert J. Canady

ISBN 0-87659-119-5 / 256 pages / 1989 / Gryphon House 10011 / PB

More Story S-t-r-e-t-c-h-e-r-s®
More Activities to Expand Children's Favorite Books (Pre-K–K)
Shirley C. Raines and Robert J. Canady

ISBN 0-87659-153-5 / 254 pages / 1991 / Gryphon House 10020 / PB

Story S-t-r-e-t-c-h-e-r-s® for the Primary Grades
Shirley C. Raines and Robert J. Canady

ISBN 0-87659-157-8 / 256 pages / 1992 / Gryphon House 10026 / PB

450 More Story S-t-r-e-t-c-h-e-r-s® for the Primary Grades
Shirley C. Raines

ISBN 0-87659-167-5 / 255 pages / 1994 / Gryphon House 15133 / PB

Available at your favorite bookstore, school supply store, or order from Gryphon House at 800.638.0928 or www.gryphonhouse.com.